IMAGES
*of America*

# Charlotte and Mecklenburg County Police

**On the Cover:** Initially the Charlotte police transported suspected criminals to the police station in a horse-drawn wagon with low sides. A ride in the Black Maria served to disgrace the arrestee in full view of their neighbors. In 1914, Chief Horace Moore convinced the city to purchase a new motorized brass-adorned Black Maria from the Ford Motor Company. However, the department's first police car was mostly used by Moore himself. (Charlotte-Mecklenburg Police Department [CMPD] Archives.)

IMAGES
*of America*

# CHARLOTTE AND MECKLENBURG COUNTY POLICE

Ryan L. Sumner on behalf of the
Charlotte-Mecklenburg Police Department
and the Charlotte-Mecklenburg
Police Benevolent Fund

ARCADIA
PUBLISHING

ISBN 978-0-7385-6671-9

Published by Arcadia Publishing
Charleston SC, Chicago IL, Portsmouth NH, San Francisco CA

Printed in the United States of America

Library of Congress Control Number: 2009933088

For all general information contact Arcadia Publishing at:
Telephone 843-853-2070
Fax 843-853-0044
E-mail sales@arcadiapublishing.com
For customer service and orders:
Toll-Free 1-888-313-2665

Visit us on the Internet at www.arcadiapublishing.com

*This book is dedicated to the men and women—sworn and non-sworn—who uphold the laws and serve the citizens of Charlotte and Mecklenburg County.*
*All offer their talent and dedication,*
*while some have given their lives in this duty.*
*They are our history.*

# CONTENTS

# Prologue

## Law Enforcement in the Old South

In the 1760s, Scots-Irish Presbyterians coming down the Great Wagon Road from Pennsylvania wrested a small village from the backwoods wilderness at the intersection of two Native American trading paths. Mecklenburg County was newly formed, and village leaders moved quickly to erect a courthouse, a jail, and stocks at their own expense to establish the settlement they had christened Charlotte Town as the seat of the county's government and legal structure.

With Charlotte Town operating as the ad hoc county seat until it was recognized by the State Assembly more than a decade later, Moses Alexander became Mecklenburg's first sheriff in 1763. The colonial sheriff dealt mainly with matters of the court, such as quit-rents and conflicts over land claims. Lawbreakers were rare in the early county records, and the sheriff little concerned himself with peacekeeping, or what is today called policing. Those duties fell to the county's two constables and were often accomplished by the citizens themselves.

The ensuing decades saw Charlotte grow more populous, and while Mecklenburg never boasted the gigantic plantations of the Deep South, slave-based cotton agriculture funded some large patrician estates, especially in the northern parts of the county. The bonded population of the county rose from 14 percent in 1790 to 40 percent in the decade before the Civil War. Though about a quarter of Mecklenburgers owned one or more slaves, only the wealthiest one percent managed large agricultural operations comprising more than 20 bondsmen. Because of large land ownership requirements for voting and holding office, this small aristocracy controlled local government until the Civil War and laid the foundation for county law enforcement agencies.

Police control of the slaves was of such concern to elite whites that the Mecklenburg County courts authored numerous ordinances and created a separate law enforcement agency specifically to regulate the bonded population. While slave catching was part of the 19th-century county constable's job, he also summoned jurors and witnesses, attended court, and kept order in the courtroom. The constabulary received a fee for any arrests they made and took a reactive approach to their law enforcement duties, not getting involved until after a crime was committed. Conversely, the sworn members of the county's slave patrol received direct payment and worked at night proactively patrolling districts, called beats, in groups of three or four at a time on horseback. Ever anxious of a revolt, the county charged the patrollers with breaking up nighttime meetings of slaves, searching their homes for guns and other weapons, stopping black market trade between blacks and poorer whites, and checking that any slaves found off the plantation had written passes giving them permission to do so. Additionally, slave patrols in the Carolinas and Virginia are credited with inventing the stakeout and were regarded by observers as being better organized than Northern watch groups. Members of the patrol had judicial power to flog blacks on the scene for infractions of the law without trial, and on occasion, the patrol could also punish whites when they violated race-related laws. Dr. J. B. Alexander recounted an 1845 Mecklenburg County raid, when a group of seven patrollers forcibly pulled a white man from the quarters of a female slave and whipped him 39 times for miscegenation. A committee, composed of three prominent men from each county district, oversaw the activities of the patrol. Although the North Carolina government authorized the formation of the slave patrols (initially called "searchers") in the 18th century, records are not clear when Mecklenburg started using them—only that the county vigorously employed them for 40 years preceding the Civil War.

Perhaps dissatisfied with the protection afforded by the county-based constables and slave patrol, Charlotte aldermen experimented with establishing their own police. On June 22, 1816, they instituted the Town Watch, composed of citizen volunteers, to patrol the town during the hours of darkness, to prevent slave gatherings, and to cut down on urban crime. Every night between 9:00 or 10:00 p.m., one of the watchmen blew a horn. Town ordinances decreed, "All negro slaves not in their homes by half an hour after the horn had blown were punished by not less than five or more than forty lashes, and the owner of the slave was fined $1.00." By 1819, Charlotte alderman divided the town into two wards, each with a captain of the watch, who assigned men of military age from his ward to patrol duty. Failure to serve resulted in a fine.

The establishment of gold mines in Mecklenburg County on Charlotte's southern outskirts in 1825 evidently troubled the city's leaders and better classes. The mines—loud and dirty places where work was dangerous—employed a desperate combination of leased slaves, poor white farmers, and foreign immigrants. A newspaper correspondent for the *New York Observer* wrote of the lawless nature of Mecklenburg's mining camps in 1831 saying, "I can hardly conceive of a more immoral community than exists around these mines . . . Drunkenness, gambling, fighting, lewdness, and every other vice exists [sic] here to an unlawful extent." Likely in response to the presence of these camps, Charlotte revisited its system of police protection in 1827, augmenting the town guard with several constables who were paid a fee for each arrest they made.

By the early 1850s, the gold rush had tapered off, and Charlotte citizens were weary of serving on watch at night. In the winter of 1852, the aldermen opened the city's coffers to employ George Plummer and nine other Town Guards at a salary of $15 per month. Like their predecessors, the guards patrolled the town from 9:00 p.m. to dawn, but additionally, they had to "cry out in a loud tone of voice" every hour saying " 'all is well' and give the time." Failure to do this netted the watchmen a $1 fine. Additionally, aldermanic edict required that the guardsmen clean and trim the wicks of the new kerosene lamps then lining Tryon Street.

The guards and county slave patrol could still be supplemented by members of the community in times of emergency. Fear of slave insurrection ran rampant in the months before the outbreak of the Civil War. Between March 29 and April 1, 1861, a group of three men set five structures ablaze in Charlotte. More than 200 men enrolled as additional patrol to act in concert with the Town Guard until the incendiaries could be apprehended. In what would prove to be the final days of the war, Mayor Samuel A. Harris, a former constable, called for the organization of "a volunteer company or companies to defend the town against raids and assaults by the enemy."

Federal control after the Civil War profoundly affected the development of policing in the county. In the war's immediate aftermath, Charlotte fell into disarray; former Confederate soldiers and war refugees filled streets and makeshift hospitals, mobs looted stores, and drunkenness and disorder abounded. The threat of racial riot was high, as large numbers of former slaves forsook the countryside for the more urban environs of Charlotte. Most townspeople welcomed the restored order brought by the arrival of federal troops. Union commanders immediately set up a system of magistrates bolstered by a civilian police company in each of the county's eight districts. The U.S. Army issued these new police captured arms and ammunition but did not compensate them monetarily for their efforts. On May 28, 1865, seventy-six Mecklenburgers took an oath of allegiance to the U.S. government and swore to "preserve the peace, prevent crime, and arrest criminals . . . and to obey all lawful orders of the U.S. Military authority." Unable to locate suitable Union men for these positions, the Federals initially pulled these new peacekeepers from the ranks of former slave owners. The following month the newly appointed mayor, Dr. H. M. Prichard, also became Intendant of Police at a $1,000 per year salary. On January 11, 1866, the city hired eight patrolmen, each paid $50 per month. Around this time, the city also began employing a secret detective, known only to the mayor.

As the initial occupation gave way to the Reconstruction, the old-line aristocrats lost power, and poor whites, Northern businessmen, and freed slaves found appointment to local government positions. Mayor Edward Bissell—a New York–born mining industrialist with an African American wife and mixed race children—further infuriated the old aristocracy by daring to appoint "two or more negroes to the police force along with some very bad white men who were no better," according to municipal records for the city of Charlotte. In fact, one of the earliest postwar demands of African Americans in the South was for police officers of their own race, especially after race riots gripped New Orleans and Memphis, and insurgent terrorists began targeting the freedmen. Between 1868 and 1875, African Americans comprised two or three of the city's eight policeman. Additionally, emancipated blacks found representation as Mecklenburg deputies and volunteered on posses organized to find dangerous criminals. In Mecklenburg, these gains proved to be short-lived.

Much changed in 1869 when martial law eased in the region, and Charlotte held elections for local offices for the first time since the war, voting a former Confederate officer as mayor and other prewar leaders into aldermanic positions. In what may have been a deliberate show of defiance to the Union occupiers and intimidation to the newly freed slaves, the new city leaders issued the Charlotte police their first uniforms:

> To be of cadet gray frock coat with straight vest and standing collar, with six brass buttons on the coat. Pants, gray. Cap, blue with black leather frontpiece upon which shall be neatly lettered City Police Ward One or Two (as the case may be). Each Policeman is to wear a black leather belt.

This rebellious choice of color may well have been to avenge returning Confederate troops who insultingly had their insignia and buttons cut off their military garments by the members of the U.S. Army occupying Charlotte. Federal troops left Charlotte in the spring of 1872.

The story that follows principally concerns the nearly 150 years between the Civil War and the present, during which time police in Charlotte and Mecklenburg County displayed tremendous courage and sacrifice in the execution of their duty, adapted to social and cultural changes within the American South, and increasingly embraced sophisticated methods and technology to meet challenges posed by criminals and a violent culture.

# *One*

# Creating a Police Force in Turbulent Times

## The Origins of Policing in Charlotte and Mecklenburg County

Modern policing in Charlotte and Mecklenburg County came into being during one of the most tumultuous periods of history. The decades that followed the Civil War brought previously unimaginable social and economic changes, including the end of slavery, postwar boomtown prosperity, shifts in political power, and rapid industrialization. Many Charlotteans hoped to build a world on forward-looking ideas—a vision they referred to as "the New South." Others desperately clung to the comfort of old ideologies. Police often found themselves in the center of this conflict.

As with other Southern institutions, police in this period struggled to redefine and reinvent their role. In Charlotte, this process involved shifting from informal police systems to more professionalized models by combining parts of their antebellum social control roles with lessons learned during federal occupation and new practices borrowed from foreign agencies.

Mecklenburg's past is surprisingly bloody. The roots of the culture of violence, which challenges police today, reaches back to the late 19th and early 20th centuries. In 1900, it was rare for one week to go by without at least one local rape, stabbing, or murder splashed across the headlines. A 60-year crime wave that began in 1900 peaked in 1940, when Charlotte earned the dubious distinction as the city with nation's highest murder rate.

Prior to the Civil War, Mecklenburg County's principle police force consisted of its slave patrol, which was charged with controlling a bonded population nearly equal in size to the free population. Patrollers enforced the numerous ordinances specifically targeting people of color. Charlotte's

Town Guards provided a similar function in the urban area. (*The Plantation Police* by Francis H. Schell, Library of Congress.)

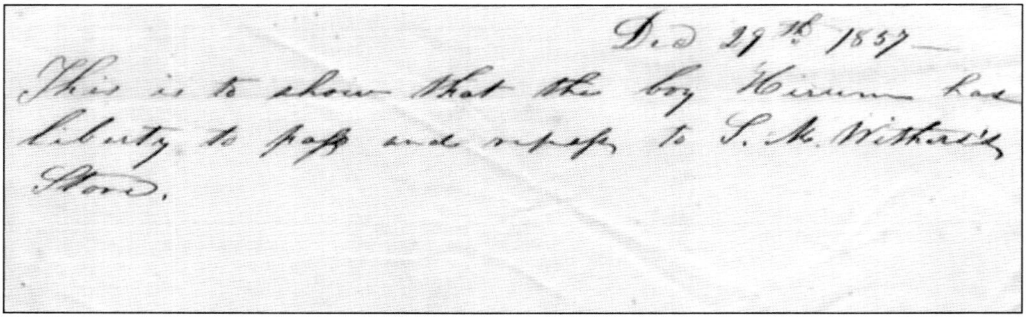

Dec 29th 1857—
This is to show that the boy Hiram has liberty to pass and repass to S. M. Withers's Store.

Anytime a slave ventured from home, the law required they carry a pass—usually a dated, handwritten, and signed note from the bondsman's owner stating where they had permission to travel. A slave needed to show the pass to any patroller who stopped them or face punishment. This 1857 Mecklenburg pass gives a slave permission travel to a store. (J. Murrey Atkins Library Special Collections Department, UNC Charlotte.)

Slaves faced extremely harsh penalties for breaking Charlotte's race-based laws, as illustrated by the following examples from the 1864 Ordinances of the Town of Charlotte: 15 lashes at the public whipping post for being "found in any dram or grog shop;" 39 lashes for attending a non-permitted "assemblage of slaves;" not less than five nor more than 39 lashes for offenders who "smoke a pipe or cigar in any street, walk with a club or bludgeon, or carry any weapon;" a night in jail followed by 25 lashes awaited slaves "found from his or her home after the hour of half-past nine o'clock p.m.;" buying or receiving alcohol as a gift carried a penalty of "whipping not to exceed thirty-nine lashes." Public whippings in Charlotte took place at the square, where the pillories stood. Federal occupation in 1865 brought an end to public whippings in Charlotte. (Public Library of Charlotte and Mecklenburg County [PLCMC], Carolina Room.)

U.S. military officials were chiefly concerned with establishing law and order in the South in the immediate aftermath of the Civil War. Although the 6,000 Union troops camped in Charlotte set up martial law, one of their first orders of business was establishing a system of courts and an armed police force composed of local Mecklenburg men. They accomplished this in May 1865. A month later, William Holden (right), North Carolina's provisional governor, appointed a local intendant over the police forces in Charlotte—the first step in returning law enforcement to the control of local government. (North Carolina Department of Archives and History.)

During Reconstruction, blacks and poor whites gained the right to vote, which resulted in the election of numerous freedmen to aldermanic and other government positions. It was also during this period that Charlotte gained its first black police officers. These gains threatened Charlotte's better classes, who began moving to block people of color out of local politics after Reconstruction ended. (Library of Congress.)

Considered by many to be the father of modern policing, British Home Secretary Sir Robert Peel founded the London Metropolitan Police in 1829 and created a system of reforms that law enforcement agencies worldwide adopted. Though the formal list of his Nine Principles is largely the creation of textbook writers, they do seem to have been gleaned from the reformer's speeches. (1900 illustration from an earlier painting by J. Wood.)

The influence of the London Metropolitan Police model is clearly visible in this 1910 photograph of Charlotte's law enforcers. The domed hats and blue uniforms, truncheon, and individually numbered badges came from Peel's reforms. The officers shown here are, from left to right, (seated) Hugh Shields, Cliff Bell, J. T. Farrington, J. D. Johnson, and B. J. Summerow; (standing) M. M. Earnhart, Charles Ayers, Lee Hargett, J. E. Crowell, and J. M. Earnhart. (PLCMC, Carolina Room.)

Another idea originating with the London Metropolitan Police was the use of wooden rattles as standard equipment. In 1880, the City of Charlotte purchased eight rattles for the police force to use on patrol. Though cumbersome, the rattle proved an ideal tool to summon aid, raise an alarm, or get people's attention. If needed, it could be used as a weapon. The police whistle, another British contribution, eventually replaced rattles.

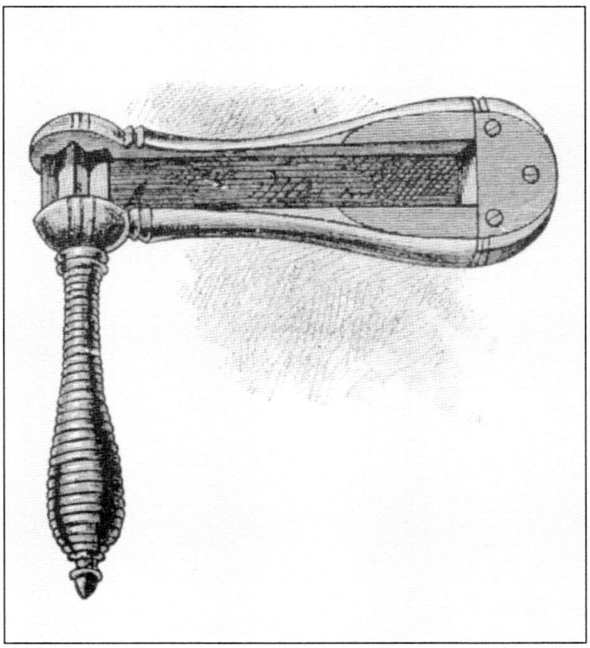

J. L. Orr
Policeman
$ 50.00
Salary for January '77
February 2d 1877

As this 1877 payroll receipt indicates, Charlotte's late-19th-century policemen earned working-class wages. This monthly salary would buy about $1,000 worth of similar goods today. The First Annual Report of the Commissioner of Labor (1885) indicates Charlotte police earned roughly the same amount as those with manufacturing jobs. Census data shows that many Charlotte police in this period started out in life as farmers and may well have appreciated the stability provided by a regular paycheck. (PLCMC, Carolina Room.)

With neither a chief nor department-issued pistols, these eight men preserved law and order in Charlotte around 1880. They are, from left to right, (seated) Major McKey, Kendrick Stephens, Henry Hill, and George Farrington; (standing) Officer Carter, Joe Orr, L. A. Blackwelder, and Mike Haley. (CMPD Archives.)

Charlotte chief of police Dick Mason and his men posed for this photograph shortly after losing their first officer in the line of duty. James Moran, a native of Ireland, was shot in April 1892 while detaining a robbery suspect at Eighth and College Streets. Aldermen ordered the town treasurer to pay his funeral expenses and the mortgage on his home. (CMPD Archives.)

In the estimation of then Mecklenburg Superintendent of Health, Dr. Charles M. Strong, Police Chief William Silas Orr (left) deserved a Congressional Medal for his actions during a severe smallpox epidemic that hit Charlotte between 1898 and 1900, infecting around 1,500 people and causing more than 100 deaths. People suspected of being infected and those with the disease were removed and segregated into different detention camps, called pest houses. Charlotte's aldermen passed an ordinance for compulsory vaccination, which fell to Chief Orr and his men to enforce. The execution of this duty brought police into conflict with Charlotte's blue-collar workers. (Charlotte Fire Department Archives.)

After inoculating children at Charlotte's segregated schools, health workers, flanked by a squad of police officers, turned to Charlotte's textile mills. Mill workers scattered for the doors and windows when police, led by Orr, entered the Gingham Mill (above). At the Victor Mill, police dragged workers resisting the vaccination to jail. In the newspaper, mill-hands voiced their concerns and feelings of being singled out, challenged whether the homes of Charlotte's elites would be so invaded, and pointed out that businesspersons working in Uptown's crowded environs could refuse the vaccine without repercussion. "If officers will commence at the square and vaccinate everybody engaged in public service within the limits of the town, then I can say with surety that when they get to the mills there will be no need for pistols or dogs," suggested one letter. (PLCMC, Carolina Room.)

After the 1903 relocation of the North Carolina Medical College to Charlotte at the southeast corner of Sixth and Church Streets (above), police began having a hard time keeping people buried. Evidently, the proximity to Elmwood Cemetery (below) proved too great a temptation for eager anatomy students who, according to one account, scarcely allowed the flowers to wilt before ghoulishly setting out with picks and shovels to replenish the cadaver cupboard. Grave robbing became such a nuisance that the alderman established a special police "death-watch patrol" to combat the problem. (Above, PLCMC, Carolina Room; below, Art Work of Charlotte.)

From left to right, Capt. J. F. Farrington, Chief H. C. Irwin, and Cliff Bell are shown on horseback around 1906. (CMPD Archives.)

The construction of the 2,600-acre Camp Greene military training facility during World War I brought 30,000 to 60,000 soldiers from all over the United States to Charlotte—a city with just over 34,000 residents. Soldiers inundated the town's saloons and brothels, no doubt posing a challenge to the city's 25 sworn police officers. The police department was able to supplement its $30,000 annual budget during this time because the military paid $50 for every AWOL (absent without leave) soldier the Charlotte police arrested and turned over to military authorities. (PLCMC, Carolina Room.)

Good Samaritan, a segregated hospital for African Americans, became the site of a heinous, and now largely forgotten, murder on August 26, 1913. On that date, patient Joe McNeely—under arrest for the shooting of police officer L. L. Wilson—convalesced from wounds incurred during a gun battle with police. At 1:30 p.m., a group of 35 masked men broke down a locked door, forced their way into the medical facility, and overpowered two police officers standing guard, even as one desperately attempted to call headquarters on the telephone. The mob hauled McNeeley, naked, from bed into the street and shot him 20 times. (PLCMC, Carolina Room.)

McNeeley's murder—the city's second lynching of an African American in three years—prompted Charlotte police to begin building an automobile fleet. Police argued that had cars been available, they might have been able to respond to the scene in time to either save McNeeley or apprehend some of the perpetrators. (CMPD Archives.)

One of the city's more sensational crimes occurred in 1926, when 19-year-old textile worker Nellie Freeman (left) nearly decapitated her husband with a straight razor. The trial became a media circus, with vendors even selling souvenir razor pins. Even though she admitted doing it, the court could not bring itself to execute a woman, so they acquitted her. Afterward, Freeman asked to keep the razor and blood-soaked dress. Pictured with Freeman is her defense attorney, Jake F. Newell. (*Charlotte Observer.*)

By 1917, Mecklenburg County required a full-time police force to replace the part-time Rural Police. Initially organized as an offshoot of the sheriff's department, the Mecklenburg County police (still often referred to as the Rural Police) became an independent department in the 1920s under the County Commission and Chief V. P. Fesperman (center). A civil-service board took over the rural force in the 1930s to remove the police function from the influence of politics. Though their resources and manpower were limited, the county's officers developed their own culture and way of doing things. They policed the unincorporated areas of the county and Mint Hill, and helped other Mecklenburg towns until the 1993 merger with the Charlotte police. (PLCMC, Carolina Room.)

# *Two*

# Earning the Badge
## The Rookie School Experience

Until the late 1930s, the training of police in Charlotte remained largely informal. Once hired and sworn in, an officer hit the streets. If lucky, the rookie worked with a training officer—rarely the same one twice—for a week or two.

Formal training programs at the Police Club, Central Piedmont Community College, and two successive facilities on Shopton Road became the academic, physical, and cultural crucibles in which new officers were forged.

During the spring of 1938, Chief Ed Pittman sponsored a "police school," conducted according to the principles recommended by the FBI National Police Academy. The program consisted of three-hour classes held once a week for a period of 12 weeks. Subjects taught included Court Procedure and Evidence, Criminal Law, Traffic, and Use of Firearms. (City of Charlotte.)

Around the time Charlotte police began adopting formal training practices, they constructed this outdoor pistol range for firearms practice. (City of Charlotte.)

In this 1940s photograph, the Charlotte police practice disarming a gun-wielding suspect. (CMPD Archives.)

Initially organized in 1947 for firearms training, the Police Club, located near Charlotte's Douglas Airport, housed the first four-week recruit school in 1953. (CMPD Archives.)

In the early 1960s, recruit school increased to six weeks and moved to Central Piedmont Community College (CPCC), where it remained until the mid-1970s. Here Prof. Perry Rivkind teaches a 1967 class of recruits a lesson in Freudian psychology. (*Charlotte Observer.*)

Here recruits learn how to work a crime scene in the mid-1960s. (CMPD Archives.)

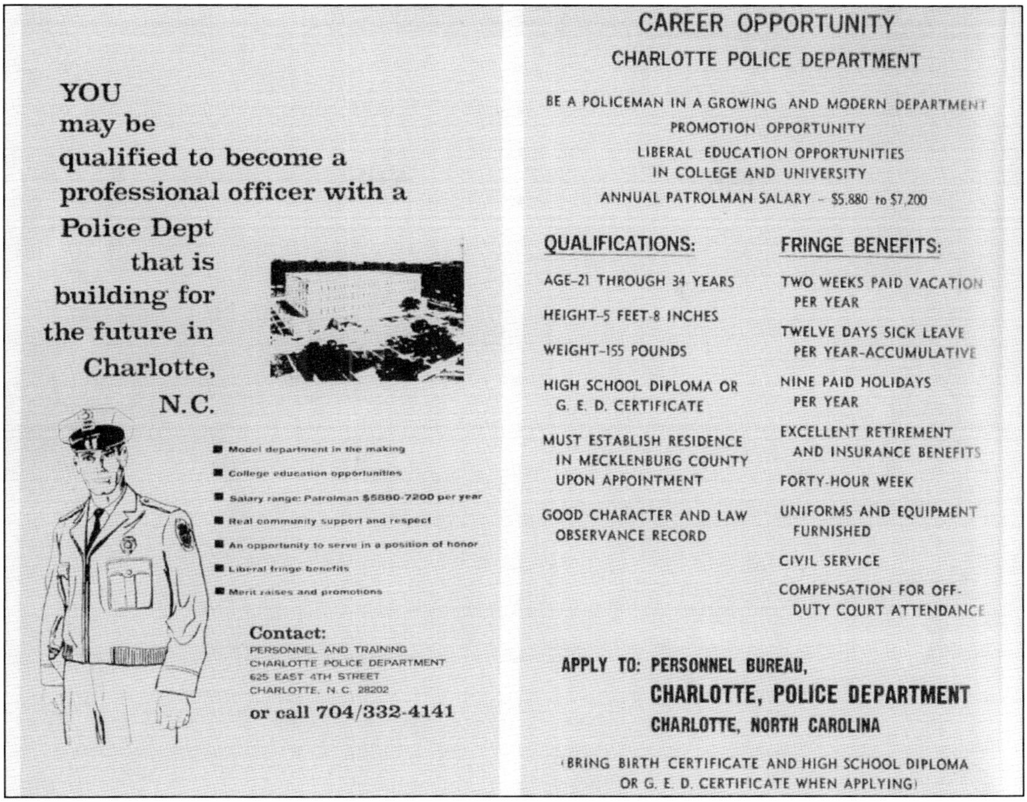


This recruitment brochure from the late 1960s and 1970s describes the necessary qualifications and fringe benefits of a career as an officer with the Charlotte Police Department. (CMPD Archives.)

By the early 1970s, city police had lost their airport facility and began to feel quite cramped at CPCC. It was around this time that the state also began regulating police education programs, which lead to the creation of the department's training bureau in 1973. A $1.3 million bond issue paid for the creation of a new Police-Fire Training Academy on Shopton Road, which opened in May 1976. Recruits from the Mecklenburg County Police and other agencies trained alongside the future Charlotte officers. (*Charlotte Observer.*)

Intense physical training, as seen here in 1981, is very much a part of the academy experience, building both strength and confidence. (*Charlotte Observer.*)

Defensive tactics instructor Chris Couch handcuffs Sgt. Howard Warren as part of a demonstration. (*Charlotte Observer.*)

The academy is also where seasoned officers take tests and attend in-service training after they are hired. Here Officer S. R. Brown takes aim during a police qualifying session in 1986. (*Charlotte Observer.*)

A recruit learns to drive backward through a figure-eight maze in 1961. (*Charlotte Observer.*)

Donald Campbell inspects his fellow recruits at the academy in 1981. Ceremonial activities such as this provide an opportunity for leadership roles as well as a way to promote steadiness, attention to detail, and group adhesion. (*Charlotte Observer.*)

Recruits Steve Greeno (left) and Paul Heyard raise the flag as part of the class's morning activities in 1981. (*Charlotte Observer.*)

Mayor Harvey Gantt addresses the Charlotte Police Training Academy's 76th recruit class, consisting of new city and county officers, in 1984. (*Charlotte Observer.*)

City clerk Lillian Hoffman swears in new officers in 1947. They are, from left to right, Harry Fisher, Officer Edwards, Don Dellinger, C. V. Purser, Herman McGowan, D. R. Thomas, Eddy "Mule" Williams, Bob House, Sam Jarvi, Pinky Stone, unidentified, Tom Ginn, and R. M. Thompson. (CMPD Archives, gift of Don Dellinger.)

From left to right, Robert Barker, unidentified, Teresa Brown, John Collins Jr., and Thomas Crowell Jr. take their oaths during the academy graduation ceremony, becoming officers in 1985. (*Charlotte Observer.*)

The 78th class president, David P. Gehrke, holds the badge he has just received; pinning on the emblem is the final symbolic act in the transition from civilian to police officer. (*Charlotte Observer.*)

# *Three*

# This Lonely Beat

## Patrol Officers

Modern technology, changes in methods, and a variety of types of vehicles have certainly influenced the job of patrolling Charlotte streets and Mecklenburg's outlying rural areas; however, the core aspects of this vital police role have remained relatively unchanged for the last century.

Patrol officers prevent criminal and delinquent behavior, identify and apprehend suspects, maintain order and public peace, diffuse volatile situations, and respond to citizens' calls for help. To the public they are the police.

And because every officer spends some time in patrol, this important, formative experience unites police across departments and generations through a common bond.

Charlotte patrolman Frank E. Ferguson directs traffic at the corner of Fourth and South Tryon Streets in the 1920s. The officer's belt and puttees (leather leggings) indicate that Ferguson was a traffic officer assigned to a motorcycle. (PLCMC, Carolina Room.)

A 1920s patrolman walks a beat near the corner of Fourth and South Tryon Streets. (PLCMC, Carolina Room.)

Patrolman P. W. Sherer purchases a cup of lemonade from this young entrepreneur in the summer of 1959. (*Charlotte Observer*.)

City patrolman Charles "Mr. Charlie" Cordell helps a *Charlotte News* paperboy cross the street in August 1959. Positive informal contacts such as this build trust between the police and members of the public. (*Charlotte Observer*.)

Each day on patrol duty begins with roll call, a meeting outlining objectives for the shift. Here Capt. S. A. Dewese conducts a 1960 roll call in the police station's basement. (*Charlotte Observer.*)

The officer on foot is little shielded from the elements. Patrolman J. W. Bowen maintains his post on a cold and wet April day in 1959. (*Charlotte Observer.*)

In an effort to curb recent acts of vandalism, Patrolman Gerald Lammonds walks a beat between 8:00 p.m. and 4:00 a.m. in Hardeeville, an area of town near Selwyn Avenue and Colony Drive. "If my presence out here is keeping it quiet, that's good. I'd rather have it that way," said Lammonds in November 1965. (*Charlotte Observer.*)

Assigned to patrol Uptown at night, officer Ike Harrison watches Trade Street in August 1975. (*Charlotte Observer.*)

Officer M. M. "Mack" Almond stood duty on the square at Trade and Tryon Streets for more than 25 years. In 1973, he commented on the experience: "I used to could tell you anything you wanted to know within a mile of the square but it's changed so much you can't keep up with it." (*Charlotte Observer.*)

Officers Mike Justice (left) and Don Penix patrol West Trade Street in Uptown during the summer of 1977. (*Charlotte Observer.*)

Occasionally patrol officers find themselves in bizarre situations. When homeowners awoke in August 1982 to find this missile-like object in the front yard of their home on Windyrush Road, they called the police. Sgt J. N. Helms examined what was determined to be an aircraft drop tank—an object he concluded must have been planted as a practical joke. (*Charlotte Observer.*)

Sgt. J. N. Helms and Officer J. R. Driggers happened upon this burglary suspect at 200 West Fifth Street. (CMPD Archives.)

In 1991, city police officers James Stitt (left) and Bill Cagle regularly walked a beat along the wall that separated the Fairview Homes Housing Project from Wayt Street. They started their patrol at twilight, when, according to the officers, "the good people go in and the bad come out." (*Charlotte Observer*.)

Charlotte officer P. M. Ensminger checks an area near Gibbs and Kenney Streets known for drug activity in August 1989. Proactive patrolling of trouble spots is more effective than randomly driving around hoping to be in the right place at the right time. (*Charlotte Observer*.)

Charlotte's first two motorcycle officers, Fred Stanton (left) and J. Paxton, began patrolling atop Harley-Davidsons in 1919, beginning the department's long relationship with that manufacturer. (CMPD Archives.)

Three members of the Charlotte Motorcycle Squad posed in front of the Firestone dealership on West Fifth Street for this 1926 advertisement for the tire manufacturer. (CMPD Archives.)

In the spring of 1958, Charlotte's motor patrolmen began transitioning from their standard hats to wearing helmets. Officers initially complained that the new headgear was too hot, but riding in the uniform cap was no picnic either, as they often caught the wind and blew off. For this reason, cycle-mounted officers often removed the wire frame from inside the hat. (*Charlotte Observer.*)

The Charlotte Police Motorcycle Drill Team performs for a crowd in July 1962. (*Charlotte Observer.*)

The city briefly strayed from its relationship with Harley-Davidson in 1966, purchasing two rugged-terrain motorcycles in response to a rash of downtown robberies. These new bikes—as demonstrated by Patrolman J. B. Clark—could avoid heavy traffic by cutting up sidewalks, down rutted alleys, and over the ties of railroad beds. "The main thing is to have men there in a moment's notice," Chief John Hord said of the new cycles. (*Charlotte Observer.*)

Motor patrolman Robert Hoagland sits atop his 1965 Harley-Davidson FLB—this was the last year for the panhead motor and the first for the electric starter. (CMPD Archives.)

The men and vehicles of the Mecklenburg County police, including their convertible Cadillac "Flyer," are pictured outside the Mint Street Jail in the late 1920s. From left to right are Jesse Dodger, Rufus Hazlewood, John Bingham, Henry Mosley, Robert Nelson Goforth, Chief V. P. Fesperman, John Watts (desk sergeant), J. Howard Wilson, and Stephen S. Rogers. (Mitchell Barnes.)

County officer Banks Mayhew keeps an eye on things from his 1946 patrol car. (Mitchell Barnes.)

Charlotte patrolman Paul Sherer (left) and Capt. Roy Phillips cruise the city looking for trouble in one of the department's Dodge patrol cars around 1951. (*Charlotte Observer.*)

Sgt. Fred Teeter drives one of the city's 1961 Fords on night patrol with Reserve Sgt. H. E. Edwards. (*Charlotte Observer.*)

Mecklenburg County chief G. A. Stephens checks in with Officer J. F. Killough at the beginning of his patrol in 1965—the year the county adopted this new seal on their cars. (*Charlotte Observer.*)

In April 1960, Charlotte chief Jesse James oversaw the purchase of this new "Black Maria" Dodge paddy wagon to pick up arrestees from patrolmen on walking beats downtown. The wagon also picked up from officers patrolling in cars, who would otherwise need to leave their zone unprotected to run a prisoner downtown. Chief James chose white, rather than the traditional hue, because "Black has such an awesome aspect about it." (*Charlotte Observer.*)

Mechanic Lynwood Reavis works to keep the city's "black and whites" rolling in October 1960. (*Charlotte Observer*.)

Officers H. P. Hollifield (left) and R. A. Bowers patrol near Freedom Drive in 1968—the first year marked units came equipped with air-conditioning. This was also the last year that city police drove black or black-and-white cars. In 1969, the department switched to blue and white. (CMPD Archives.)

Seventeen-year veteran Patrolman Bill Sellers surveys his beat. As a member of the Adam One team in the mid-1970s, Sellers and 41 other officers worked to cover a 1.5-mile area centered on the intersection of Trade and Tryon Streets. Before being given a patrol car, Sellers spent two years walking the beat at the square—one block each way, eight hours per shift, five shifts per week. (*Charlotte Observer.*)

Patrol officer Debbie Wong gets out of her patrol car in the spring of 1975 to speak to some young residents of Charlotte's Hidden Valley neighborhood. "I like . . . to talk to the kids," she said. "They are the forgotten people. But I might just have gotten started talking to them when some grown-up will say, 'Get away from that police car!'" (*Charlotte Observer.*)

Patrolman R. A. Bowers rounds a corner in his squad car in 1980. That year Charlotte police patrolled 1,375 miles of road in the 138-square-mile city. (*Charlotte Observer.*)

Officer Rick Grubb uses a video camera to tape a traffic arrest in January 1988. It was around this time that the Mecklenburg County police started experimenting with cameras mounted in patrol cars. (*Charlotte Observer.*)

The department's first aircraft, a Bell-47, takes off from the roof of police headquarters in the early 1970s. Originally known as the Airborne Support Bureau, the city's Aviation Unit formed in 1971, created largely through the federal Law Enforcement Assistance Administration grant program. Initially, the department trained three patrolmen for duty in this unit, growing it to six within the first three months of operation. These officers worked in rotation, so the unit was staffed seven days per week, covering 20 hours of the day. (CMPD Archives.)

In the spring of 1971, the police held a contest to name the helicopter. These two youngsters, along with 12 others, submitted the name Snoopy—a moniker the aviation crews still use to refer to their airships. The hangar at the airport became known as the doghouse. (*Charlotte Observer*.)

Snoopy boosted a 3.9-million candlepower light capable of piercing the darkest night, as illustrated by this 1973 demonstration at the Government Plaza. (*Charlotte Observer.*)

Snoopy II assists units on the ground responding to a house break-in off Shasta Lane on the morning of March 10, 1981. The department purchased Snoopy II, a Bell-206B Jet Ranger, in 1976 to replace the out-of-production Bell-47, for which it was becoming difficult to find parts. (*Charlotte Observer.*)

In 1990, the four-man and one-feline crew of Snoopy II received an award for flying more than 10,000 hours without an accident. They are, clockwise from the top, pilot Mark Brooks, observer Sam Brown, mechanic-observer David Nowlan, pilot Phil Hollifield, and hangar cat Rotor. As of 2009, the unit is still incident free. (*Charlotte Observer.*)

As of 2009, the Aviation Unit consisted of two Bell-407 helicopters, the third and fourth ships to fly for the department. These aircraft are equipped with the latest crime-fighting technology, such as GPS, night-vision, FLIR thermal imaging sensors, and lights so bright they can effectively turn night into day. (CMPD Archives.)

The psychological effect of the helicopter reduces the chances of suspects resisting arrest or fighting with the officers on the ground, thereby dramatically increasing their safety. (CMPD Archives.)

Two officers from the Mecklenburg County police's river patrol start their patrol of the Catawba River in 1957. Two years later, work began on the dam that would create Lake Norman, flooding homes, family farms, and even whole towns, such as Long Island, a North Mecklenburg community that boasted three textile mills. (*Charlotte Observer.*)

Mecklenburg County patrolman R. E. "Eddie" Prince of the Lakes Division and an unidentified officer dock one of the department's two new boats in June 1981. (*Charlotte Observer.*)

Officers Howard Nivens (front) and John Robbins (rear) tested the reception of horse-mounted patrol in October 1973. The public "reacted real well," according to Nivens and Robbins, but the department has elected not to put officers on horses due to the high costs, limited usage, and other logistics of implementing such a program. (CMPD Archives.)

Although Charlotte police began using bicycles to patrol the town in 1914, they seemed to have given them up after a few years. Officers John Diggs (left) and Tony Crawford inaugurated the city's return to bicycle-mounted patrol on June 15, 1991, when they rolled these 21-speed bikes out on their patrol of Uptown and Fourth Ward. The new program sought to bring higher police visibility and quicker response time in the center city. Today about 200 certified bike officers use bikes on patrol in Uptown and residential neighborhoods throughout the county. (*Charlotte Observer.*)

Beginning in 2007, CMPD began using Segway Personal Transporters to patrol large crowds and to keep watch in parks, greenways, shopping centers, and high-crime areas. The vehicles raise the officer 8 inches off the ground and quietly move them at two- to three-times a walking speed. (CMPD Archives.)

These 21-foot-high mobile Sky Watch towers saw use beginning in 2007 to monitor large crowds, spot disturbances, and direct officers on the ground. The towers are used at special events such as Speed Street, the Fourth of July, and New Year's Eve, as well as for surveillance of crime-prone areas. Spotlights, floodlights, loudspeakers, and a blue light attached to the cabin can quickly seize a crowd's attention. (CMPD Archives.)

# Four

# Fighting to Serve
## African American Police Officers

Although African Americans comprised 20 to 40 percent of Charlotte's police force during Reconstruction, they soon vanished as white elites moved to lock people of color out of local politics and effectively disfranchise them throughout the region.

Throughout the South, in the late 1930s and 1940s, black communities again began to ask for officers of their own race. In Charlotte, local minority leaders worked with the city to select the most capable and qualified men for the job. Thus, African American police hired in the 1940s tended to be more qualified and have higher educational attainment than their white counterparts.

Black police sued the city for equitable representation in the 1970s, pressured for more minority officers on the force and in ranking positions through the 1980s and 1990s, and eventually saw the appointment of the department's first African American chief in 2008.

In the late 1930s, WBT radio commentator Dr. Nathaniel Tross (pictured here) and other local African American leaders formed the Community Crusaders, an organization "founded for the purpose of combating crime in the Negro sections." The group successfully lobbied the city to reinstitute black officers, arguing that it would forge a new bond between police and the black community and ease racial tensions stirred by complaints of police brutality. (Levine Museum of the New South, WBT Collection.)

On July 11, 1941, the department hired A. M. "Bub" Houston (left), the first officer of color to serve on the force in at least 60 years. James Ross (right) joined the force a few months later after continued political pressure and protests by black community leaders. Houston, Ross, and a handful of officers hired after them served as "Special Peace Officers," having neither civil service protection nor sidearms. (*Charlotte Observer.*)

Civil service protection came in June 1947, after the Veterans Welfare Association of Charlotte, an organization of African American's who served during World War II, pushed for the change. Charlotte's first full-status black police officers memorialized the occasion by posing on the steps of the department headquarters. They are, from left to right, (first row) Ray Booton, Vardry Spencer, George T. Nash Jr., and James Taylor; (second row) John Lyles, James Ross, A. M. Houston, and John Hoffman. (Booton family.)

Officer Ray Booton patrolled in Charlotte's Brooklyn neighborhood when this 1947 photograph was taken. Until the early 1950s, African American officers could only work in black neighborhoods and could not arrest white suspects. They received hand-me-down uniforms and equipment, and, in some cases, bought their own service weapons. (Booton family.)

Rudy Torrence (second row, second from the left) joined the Charlotte police in 1955, around the time this photograph was made. He later became president of the North State Law Enforcement Organization, a black police professional group that sued the department in 1971 for discrimination. A 1974 federal court order settled the suit and mandated 20 percent of patrol officers and sergeants be minorities. The suit opened the doors for a whole new generation of officers. (CMPD Archives.)

Today the department's commitment to diversity hiring remains strong. In 2007, African Americans made up 17 percent of the department, with Latinos and Asians comprising 3 percent and 2 percent, respectively. Since the mid-1970s, numerous officers of color have earned the ranks of sergeant, lieutenant, captain, and major. Some have held positions close to the department's top office; Ellison Laney became the first minority deputy chief (then called commander) in 1988, followed by Nina Wright in 2001, and Kerr Putney in 2007. However, a minority officer would not hold the top executive position until 2008, when the city hired former Richmond Police Department chief Rodney Monroe (above). (CMPD Archives.)

# *Five*

# Breaking and Entering the Boys' Club

## Female Police Officers

It may come as a surprise to many that Charlotte hired its first female officers before the Great Depression. While few, these early pioneers did important work inside the department. However, opportunities for women in the department shrank greatly after male veterans of World War II began returning to Charlotte.

In the late 1960s, the city again began hiring women as officers. These jobs consisted largely of social service roles in which women had to meet higher educational standards than their male counterparts, were restricted to special units and bureaus, and were denied access to promotional exams as well as the formative police experience of street patrol. While on the job, these officers dealt with sexual harassment and worked to earn the confidence of their male peers.

Changing national trends and the efforts of several key female police officers led to attitudinal changes and reduced gender bias on the force.

Officer Eloise Brown joined the Charlotte police in 1925 as a member of the Detective Bureau. Records from the period also credit Brown as a fingerprint expert several years before the department established its Identification Bureau. She headed up a License Bureau and became assistant clerk of court. During World War II, Brown worked as a department dispatcher and a desk sergeant—roles she gave up when the international conflict ended. Brown finished her career as the chief secretary in the Traffic Division. Other women on the force at the time included Amalie "Tilley" Wallnau and Stella "Pat" Patterson. (CMPD Archives.)

*She Doesn't Look Like A Cop!*

***WOMAN RECRUIT***

**22, Blonde, 5-8, Cute**

Known for his progressive ideas, Chief John Ingersoll started hiring women as sworn officers, beginning with Gail Sloan in the spring of 1967. The *Charlotte Observer* seemed more preoccupied with Sloan's statuesque physical appearance than the fact that female candidates had to hold college degrees when the men did not or that they faced more extensive background checks. Sloan attended the academy with three other women and became an investigator in the Youth Bureau, eventually retiring as a captain. (*Charlotte Observer.*)

Before 1973, women on the Charlotte force all worked in plainclothes and could not wear slacks on duty. Thus, when local police went out in force to maintain order after Martin Luther King's assassination in April 1968, Officers Mickey Casey (left) and Gail Sloan (right) performed this duty in riot gear and skirts. (CMPD Archives.)

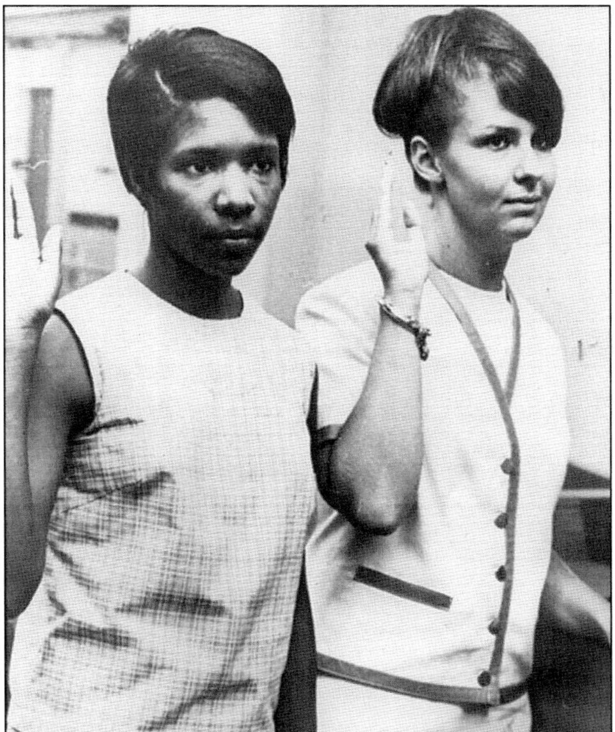

Annie Montgomery Gillespie, the department's first African American female, graduated from the academy with Cheryl Horner in July 1968. (Cheryl Horner.)

Officer Jean Larson keeps a keen eye out for trouble as she patrols in the Adam One District in 1977. Larson became the first female officer to perform patrol duty, beginning in 1973. Previously hired female officers went straight into specialized units after the academy, which bred resentment from male officers who spent years on the force before even being able to apply for such assignments. Also, the lack of experience on the street limited women's promotional opportunities and cut them out from much of the culture of policing. In 1979, Larson became the department's first female sergeant. (*Charlotte Observer.*)

By the mid-2000s, women accounted for about 14 percent of Charlotte-Mecklenburg's sworn officers and served even in the most traditionally male areas, such as SWAT. In 2004, twenty-three CMPD women held the rank of sergeant, eight were captains, one was a major, and one was a deputy chief. (CMPD Archives.)

# *Six*

# Behind the Yellow Tape
## Investigating Crime

Police attempt to prevent as much illegal activity as possible. However, once a criminal act occurs, they begin the process that will hopefully lead to the arrest of the perpetrator or perpetrators.

Police investigations usually begin by talking to people—conducting interviews and taking reports. They, or specially trained civilians, search the crime scene for evidence, ensuring that evidence is collected in the best way possible before being subjected to scientific scrutiny.

Police do not solve every crime they investigate. When they do, it is through hard work and carefully built cases.

G. W. Painter (right) and another plainclothes detective interview Onie Tadlock, while Officers L. A. Whitmore (far left) and G. W. Hollen work on their reports of a March 14, 1970, robbery. (*Charlotte Observer*.)

Officer J. R. Yates investigates the 1977 burglary of a home at 1302 North Brevard Street. The victim offered, "If you catch him, I'll give you $500." Yates replied, "The city pays me; give it to your church." (*Charlotte Observer*.)

A Charlotte officer speaks with passersby, while another secures a murder scene in the summer of 1979. (*Charlotte Observer.*)

Not all interviews are conducted in the field. Sometimes officers take witnesses or suspects to other locations for questioning. (*Charlotte Observer.*)

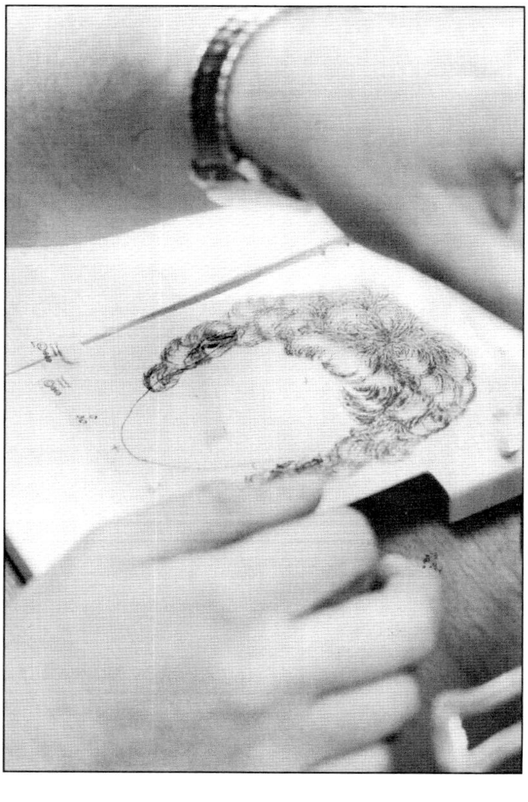

County officer I. N. Dennis takes a report from Joe McClain, who courageously pulled a man from a 1980 fire. (*Charlotte Observer.*)

Charlotte police artist Steve E. Jolly prepares a sketch in 1974. Sketches such as this, based on eyewitness descriptions, are distributed to the relevant law enforcement divisions and often to the media as a way to inform the public. (*Charlotte Observer.*)

Two Mecklenburg County officers investigate tool marks left by a home burglar on a doorway in 1963. (*Charlotte Observer.*)

City policeman R. B. Hood investigates blood spatters found on the steps of a home located at 2129 Colony Road in January 1964. The home was near the sight of a high school brawl, but Officer Hood concluded the blood was from an animal, not a human. (*Charlotte Observer.*)

Officer L. F. Matkins dusts for fingerprints on a stolen car used in the February 1983 armed robbery of a Wachovia branch bank at 3665 East Independence Boulevard. Police arrested a suspect that afternoon. (*Charlotte Observer.*)

Identification officer Ed Pierczynski examines a cache of cash drawers discovered in the woods by a young child in 1968. (*Charlotte Observer.*)

Mecklenburg County police examine a Volkswagen Beetle pulled from the woods off York Road in 1981. The car contained the badly decomposed body of a woman missing for three months. Whether police would treat this incident as an accident or a homicide was contingent on a report from the Mecklenburg County medical examiner. (*Charlotte Observer.*)

Mecklenburg sergeant W. E. Stegall (left) and Patrolman J. E. Neese make a plaster cast of a tire track as part of a murder investigation conducted in November 1975. (*Charlotte Observer.*)

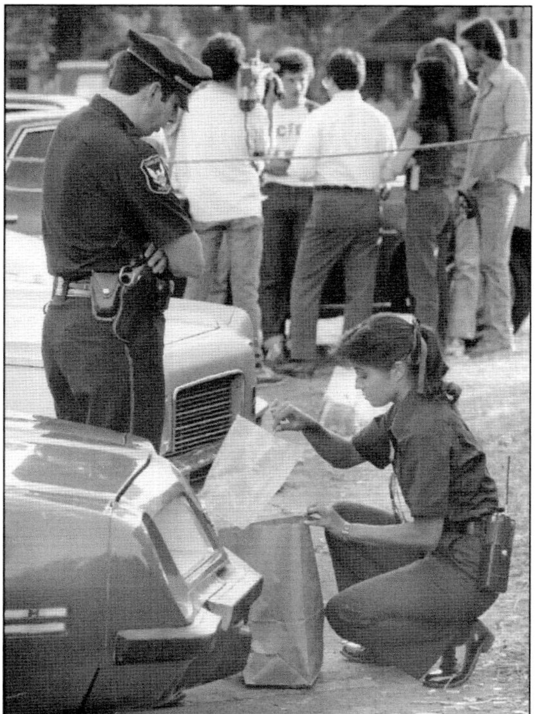

Crime scene investigator E. L. Ginn collects evidence from the scene of a suspected homicide on Sunnyside Drive in the winter of 1990. (*Charlotte Observer.*)

R. A. Gravley, an investigator with the Crime Scene Division, bags evidence at the location of a 1983 fatal shooting outside of Bedford's Lounge, while a local TV news crew conducts interviews beyond the perimeter. (*Charlotte Observer.*)

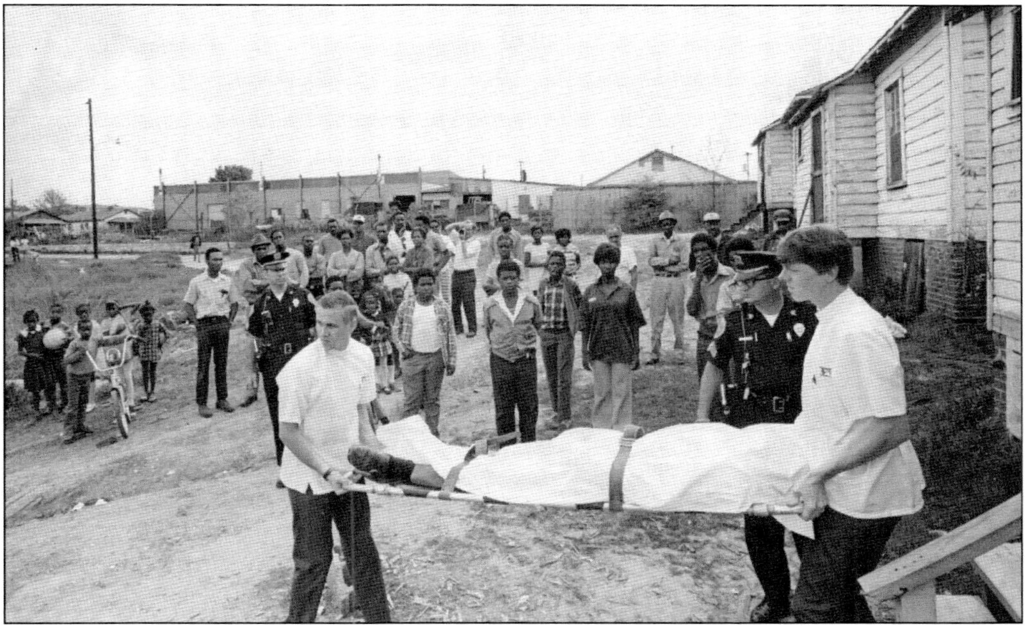

Police supervise the removal of the body of a man murdered at 2635 South Tryon Street on April 27, 1971. (*Charlotte Observer.*)

A policeman responds to the scene moments after Rodessa Wall, a member of a local black militant group, was killed by a shotgun blast during an argument on South Church Street. Police found and charged a suspect with the murder. (*Charlotte Observer.*)

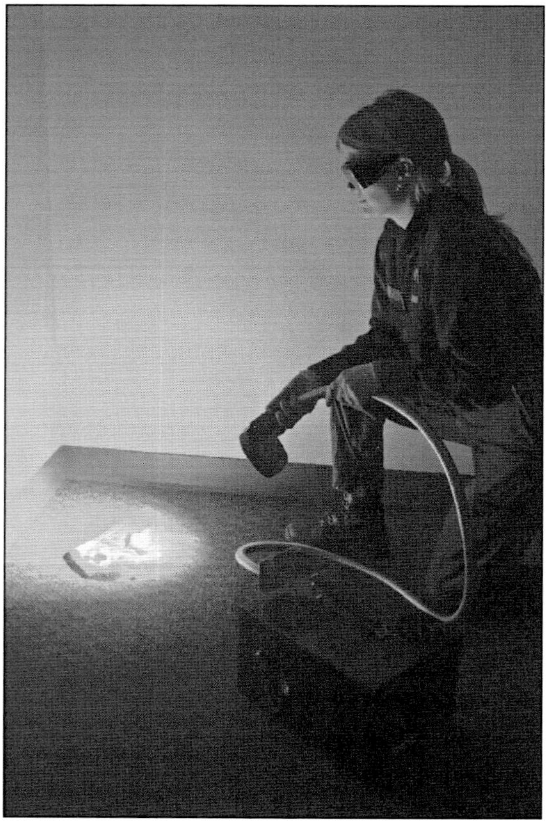

Charlotte chief Jesse James (right) and coroner W. M. Summerville examine the scene of the murder of a local cab driver. The body has been moved to the ground so that the car may be inspected for evidence. (*Charlotte Observer.*)

A CMPD crime scene investigator uses a blue alternative light source (ALS) and orange glasses to search for evidence. Many bodily fluids, organic materials, and fibers will fluoresce under ALS. Blood, gunshot residue, and some inks will absorb blue light and appear dark. These materials may be invisible to the naked eye, especially if the surface has been wiped down or cleaned. (CMPD.)

Sylvia Ferguson, a Charlotte Police Department Crime Lab technician, uses a camera to document evidence while searching the contents of a car allegedly used in a June 1993 homicide. (*Charlotte Observer.*)

Charlotte police investigator Larry Walker points crime scene search officer J. A. Welborn toward something he wants photographed as evidence during the investigation of a grocery store robbery, which resulted in the hit-and-run of a Charlotte police officer. (*Charlotte Observer.*)

County patrolman Burden drags a Mecklenburg waterway, searching for a murdered infant in March 1956. (*Charlotte Observer.*)

Under the direction of Sgt. Pete Toomey (center), Charlotte police divers Bud Cesena (right) and Ron Simmons (left) roll into the cold and murky waters of Lake Wylie, just below the Buster Boyd Bridge, in search of the handgun used in an October 10, 1982, homicide. Police charged two individuals with the murder. (*Charlotte Observer.*)

Police diver Ron Simmons participates in a 2.5-hour search of Mountain Island Lake for a safe stolen in the summer of 1984 from Nickleby's Restaurant. Police charged two men with safecracking, store breaking, and larceny. (*Charlotte Observer.*)

In January 1986, the Charlotte Scuba Team recovered this car, containing the body of Charles Richard Betchler stuffed in the trunk. Betchler's family believed he was killed because he worked as a police informant. (*Charlotte Observer.*)

Under innovative Chief Ed Pittman, the city police created the Identification Bureau in 1930—a giant leap forward in the application of scientific principles for solving crime. The new bureau occupied a small annex in city hall and had "new cameras with different lenses for different phases of crime investigations, a photostatic machine for copying records and documents, an enlarger and reducer of photographs and fingerprints, a comparison microscope for comparing bullets, shells, etc." (Pierczynski family.)

The department brought in Officer John Pierczynski, an FBI-trained identification specialist who began his law enforcement career in South Carolina, to work in the new bureau. (Pierczynski family.)

# *Seven*

# Using Science to Solve Crimes
## The Crime Lab

By the late 1960s, the Charlotte Police Department needed more and better services than the Identification Bureau could provide. All evidence requiring scientific analysis was packed up and sent to the State Bureau of Investigation's lab in Raleigh or the FBI's lab in Washington, D.C.—a lengthy process where the city would have to wait in line behind other agencies.

The successful passage of a bond issue lead to the construction of a new Law Enforcement Center in 1969, which included a new scientific facility—the only complete city crime lab in the Carolinas. The lab analyzes firearms, tool marks, shoe impressions, and suspect documents, as well as substances such as hair, blood, and narcotics.

In the late 1990s, the Charlotte-Mecklenburg Police Department established the state's first local police DNA lab to analyze bodily fluids—blood, semen, and saliva—that could identify a suspect or an unknown victim. The lab is tied into local, state, and national databases.

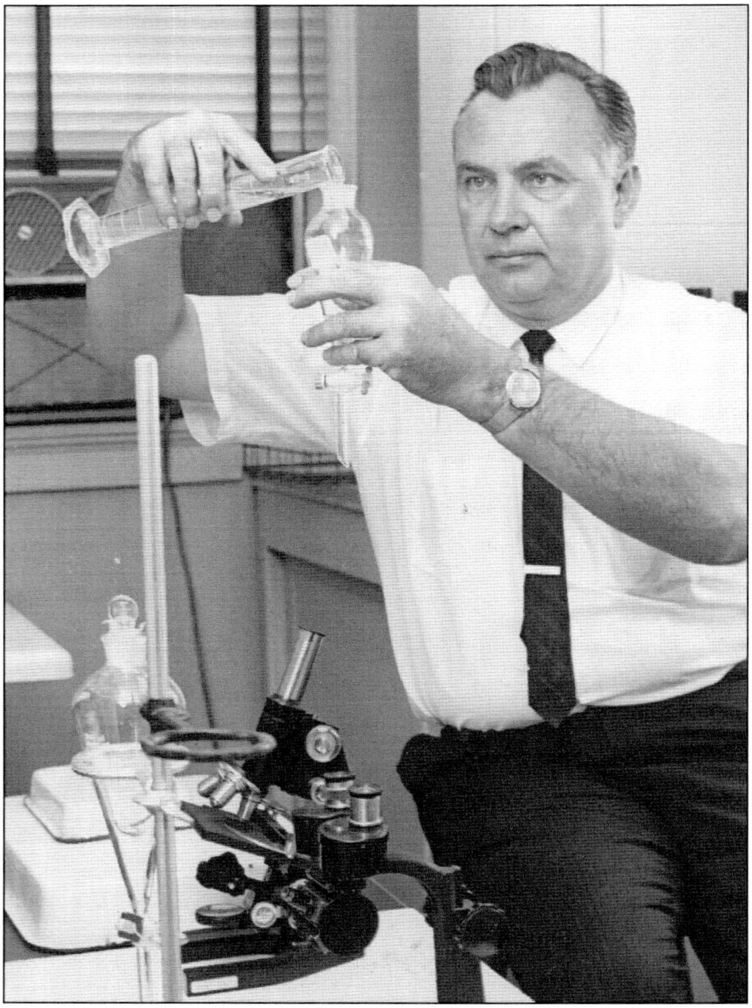

The Charlotte police hired Vincent Seavers as the founding director of the Charlotte Crime Lab in 1968. An industrial chemist by training, Seavers turned to law enforcement activities after an accident injured his hands. He was assistant director of Miami's Dade County Crime Lab before returning to his native Charlotte to set up the new facility. (*Charlotte Observer*.)

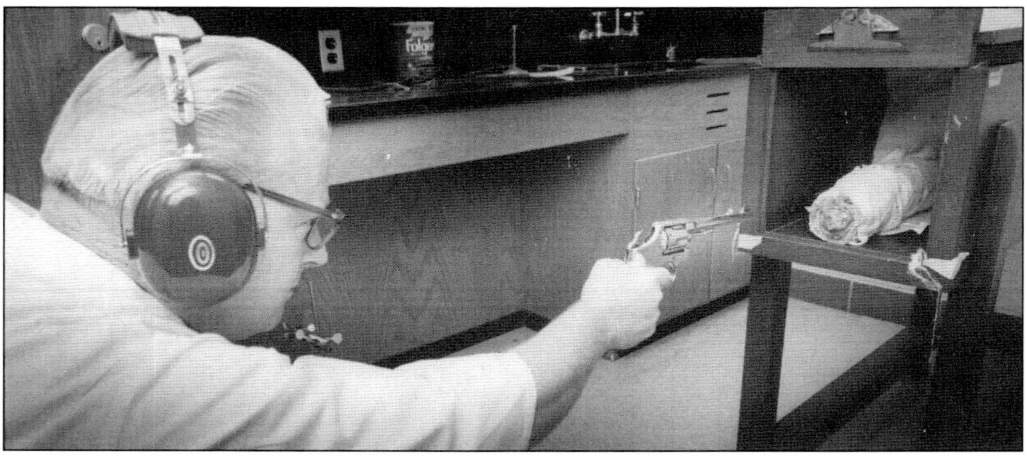

Firearms expert Cleon Mauer fires a revolver into cotton wadding to obtain a sample in 1973. Such samples are often collected for comparison against ballistic evidence found at a crime scene. (*Charlotte Observer*.)

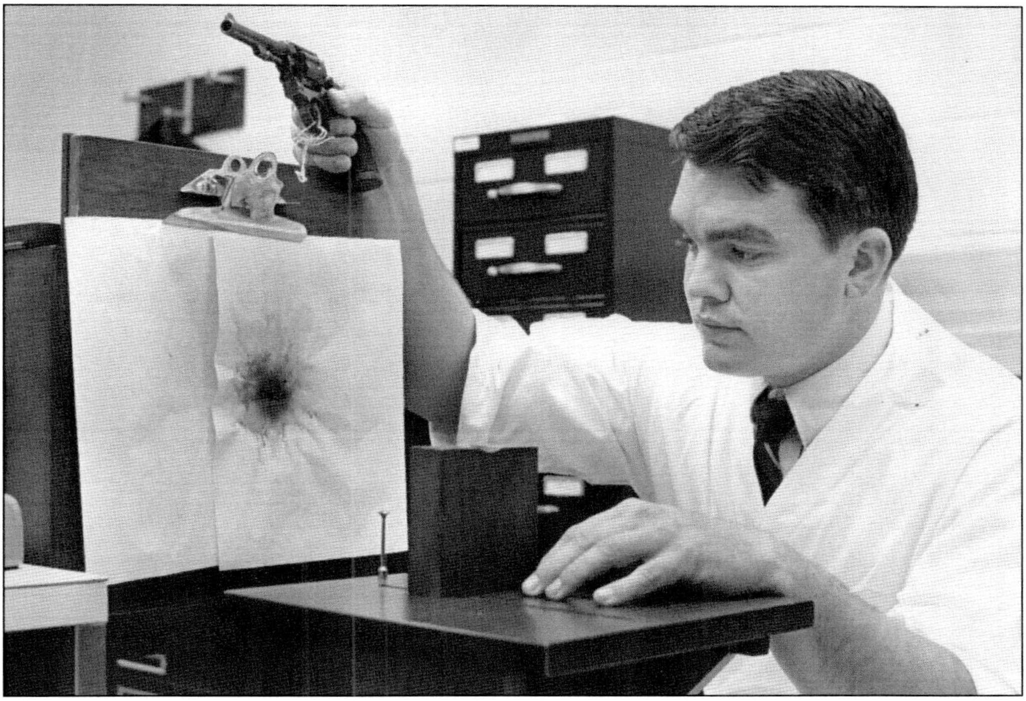

James Brietenstein creates a powder burns sample at the Charlotte Crime Lab in 1969. (*Charlotte Observer.*)

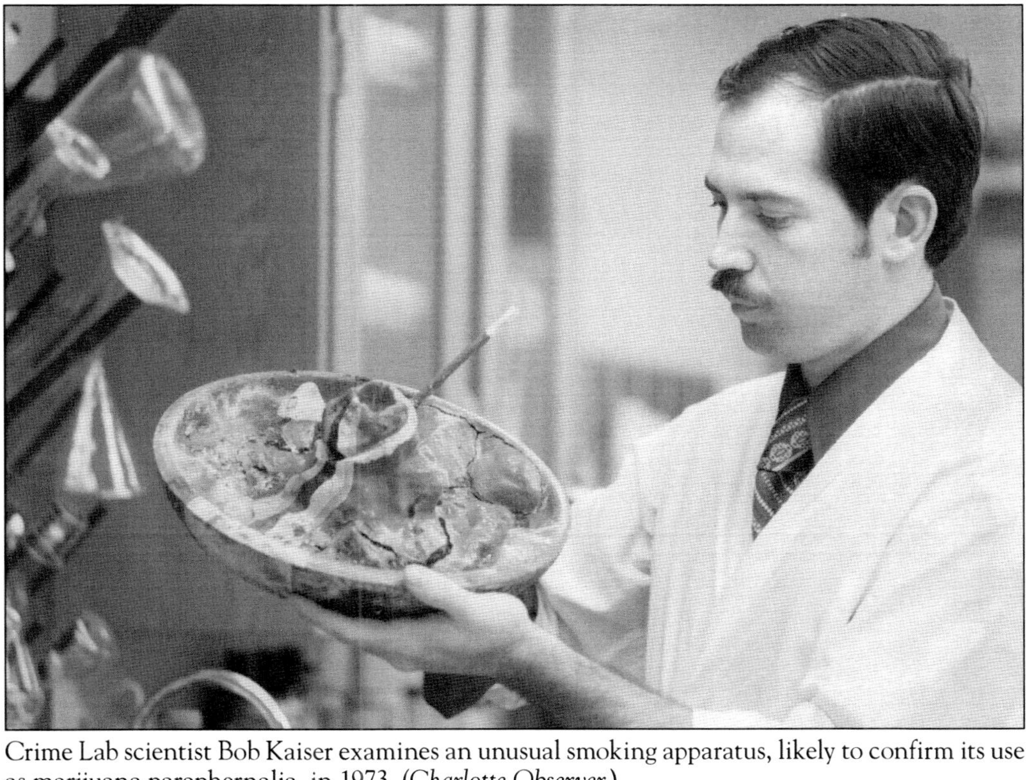

Crime Lab scientist Bob Kaiser examines an unusual smoking apparatus, likely to confirm its use as marijuana paraphernalia, in 1973. (*Charlotte Observer.*)

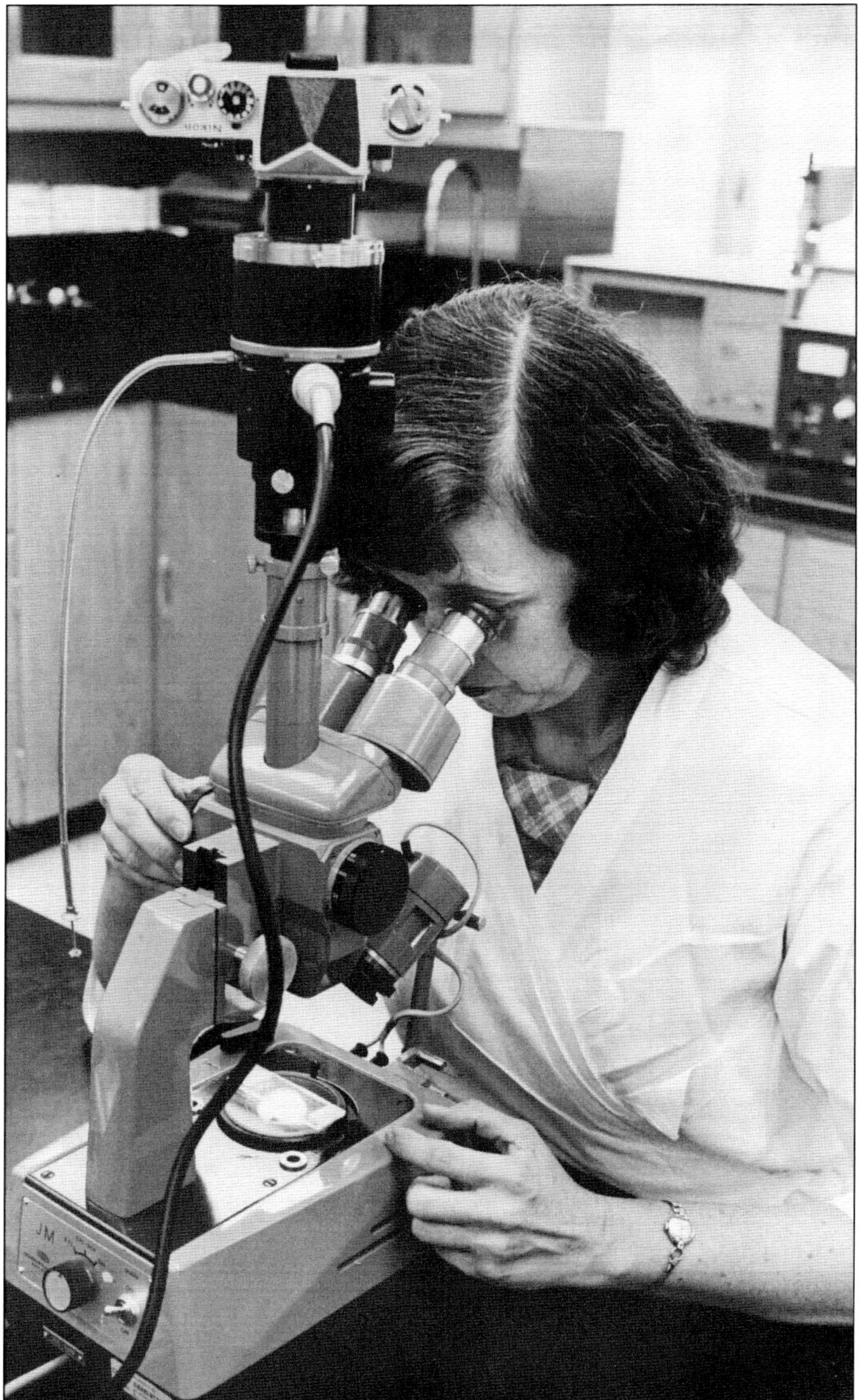

Chemist Mary Jane Burton uses a camera-enabled microscope to photograph evidence in 1971. Burton worked in cancer research before joining the Charlotte Police Crime Lab. At the time, she was the facility's sole female scientist. (*Charlotte Observer.*)

Identification expert M. G. Stubbs feeds information into a computer in hopes of matching fingerprints in 1973. (*Charlotte Observer.*)

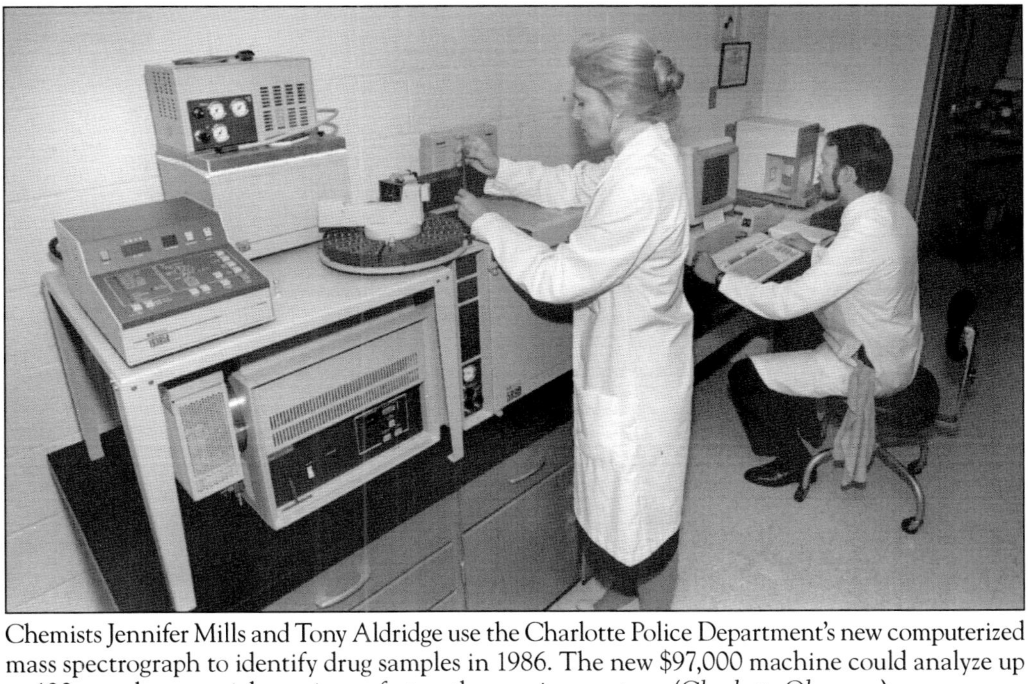

Chemists Jennifer Mills and Tony Aldridge use the Charlotte Police Department's new computerized mass spectrograph to identify drug samples in 1986. The new $97,000 machine could analyze up to 100 samples overnight, twice as fast as the previous system. (*Charlotte Observer.*)

Back at the lab, Sylvia Ferguson lifts latent fingerprints from a soda can that crime scene search technicians collected in the field in 1993. (*Charlotte Observer.*)

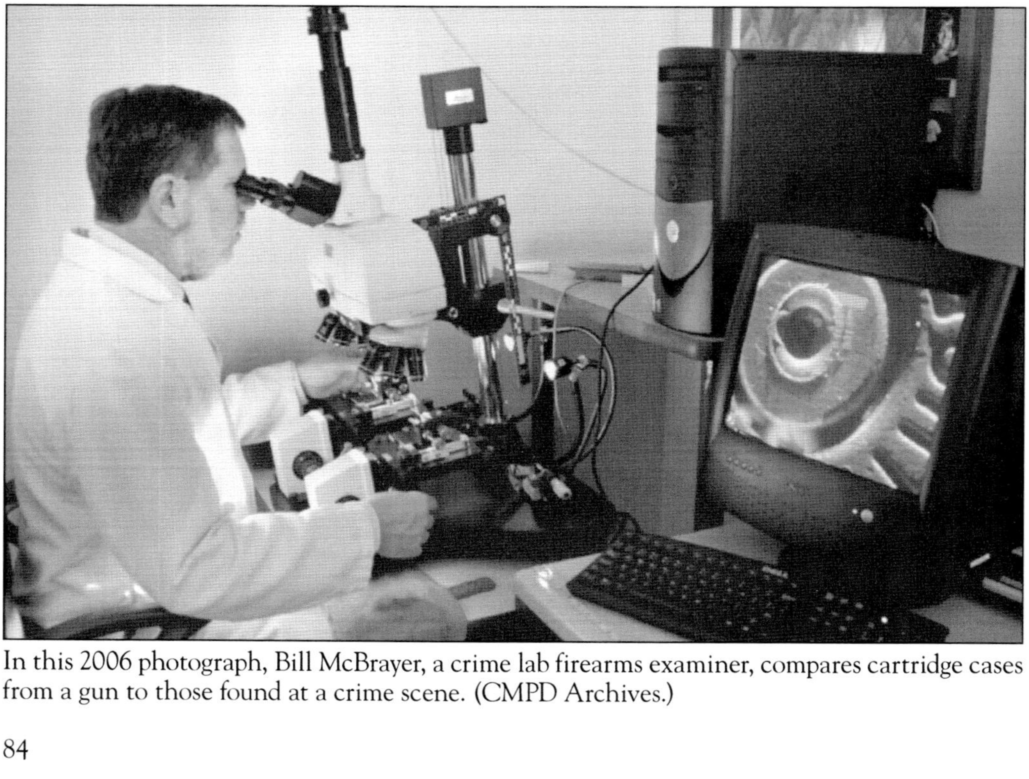

In this 2006 photograph, Bill McBrayer, a crime lab firearms examiner, compares cartridge cases from a gun to those found at a crime scene. (CMPD Archives.)

# *Eight*

# Run 'Em Downtown

## Police Headquarters

Though it has evolved and changed over the years, a main downtown police headquarters building has ever been the nerve center for the city and county's law enforcement efforts.

Even in today's era of decentralized patrol, with most units operating out of smaller, nearly autonomous team offices spread throughout the county, the downtown headquarters remains the hub around which everything revolves.

Despite Charlotte's phenomenal post–Civil War growth, the 11-man police force constituted nearly all of the city's paid employees, and the town leaders felt little need for a city hall even into the 1880s. Instead, the city rented offices and meeting space above this restaurant, then located at the northwest corner of Tryon and Sixth Streets. (PLCMC, Carolina Room.)

By 1891, Charlotte needed a real city hall. The municipal government had begun to provide more services, such as professional fire companies, water and sewer, public health, building inspection, street paving, electricity, telephone lines, garbage cremation, and a growing police force. Taxpayers funded the construction of this impressive brownstone structure on the corner of Fifth and North Tryon Streets. This stylish edifice would house the city police and city jail for most of the next four decades. (PLCMC, Carolina Room.)

Sooner than anyone expected, the city outgrew its Victorian city hall and brought in prominent local architect Charles Hook in the mid-1920s to come up with something new. Hook's vision was of civic campus to be anchored by a city hall spaced far enough from the street to accommodate future expansion. The fire (right) and police (left) departments would be housed in their own separate facilities. The location of the three new buildings, adjacent to the existing courthouse, began the creation of Charlotte's government district. (PLCMC, Carolina Room.)

From the mid-1920s to the mid-1960s, Charlotte tripled in size, and its police department quadrupled. Given this growth, it was not long before the police began to feel cramped in their headquarters building at 625 East Fourth Street, above. Much of the equipment—especially in the crime laboratory and communications room—had become obsolete. These problems, when added to several others, prompted the request for a new facility, put forth as a bond issue. The citizens responded favorably, approving money to construct a new central headquarters. (*Charlotte Observer.*)

The Charlotte Police Department moved into its new Law Enforcement Center (LEC) at 825 East Fourth Street in July 1969. The new facility boasted upgraded communications and modern crime laboratory facilities, as well as 78,000 square feet of heated space to accommodate growth and, according to the dedication booklet, "be as functional . . . in the year 2000 as it is today." (CMPD Archives.)

To make way for the construction of a new Mecklenburg County Jail in the mid-1990s, Charlotte police abandoned their East Fourth Street headquarters for their current facility that opened in August 1996 at 601 East Trade Street, pictured above. A major portion of the costs were born by the county as part of the land swap agreement and were part of the city-county police consolidation process. (CMPD Archives.)

# *Nine*

# Calling All Cars

## Communications

Police communications personnel are the lifeline between citizens needing emergency help and officers in the field. The job requires patience, skill, and a fastidious attention to detail.

Because the clearance rate of crime goes up as the response time of patrol units is reduced, communications is an area where increasing technological advances have been especially pronounced during the last century.

Jasper Stowe "Dick" Mason, chief of the department from 1891 to 1894, began the city police communications program when he oversaw the installation of the department's first telephone and authorized the hiring of a "responsible man" to answer it and look after the office at a salary of $30 per month. Not until 1926 did the department feel it necessary to purchase a second telephone line. (CMPD Archives.)

In 1929, Chief Horace Moore upgraded the city police's communication system, authorizing the installation of a PBX (private branch exchange) switchboard to replace the department's two telephones. Here Floyd Polson works the department's PBX in the mid-1950s. (CMPD Archives.)

In late 1930, the department began experimenting with broadcasting radio signals from police headquarters to patrol units in the field. The city installed a 250-watt shortwave broadcasting station, WPDV, in police headquarters but had to wait more than a year and a half before funds were available to start installing receivers in the department's patrol cars. By 1934, eight of the city's 11 police cars had the receivers. WPDV also helped the Mecklenburg County police and the fire department expedite their services. Initially, all radio communication flowed one-way from the dispatcher to units in the field. (City of Charlotte.)

The city police began experimenting with two-way radio communication in 1937, and by 1939, all officers in department cars could talk directly with headquarters. (City of Charlotte.)

In the mid-1950s, Officer Gerald "The Jinx" Gardner served as the department's lone radio dispatcher, directing 10 or 12 police cars, wreckers, and ambulances. He also answered the telephones, kept a log, and did paperwork. According to Gardner (seen here in 1961), "You might outrun a police car, but you can't outrun that radio. Sooner or later, somebody's going to be ahead of you." The Jinx heard and saw it all during his long career, eventually becoming supervisor of a much larger and technologically advanced communications center by the early 1970s. (*Charlotte Observer.*)

Civilian dispatcher L. P. Dellinger (left) works with Patrolman J. A. Nichols in the radio switchboard room of police headquarters in 1958. Although the city began employing civilians in the late 1930s as clerks and secretaries, the employment of non-sworn personnel in communications proved controversial; sworn officers handled this work until the 1970s. Some argued that dispatch required a patrolman's understanding of police work to know what information officers needed in the field. Eventually, the department decided that civilian dispatchers worked as effectively, freed police to work the streets, and cost less. By the close of the 1970s, communications had become completely civilianized. (*Charlotte Observer.*)

Although cumbersome by today's standards, Charlotte officers were grateful to have this new Motorola Handie-Talkie radio in 1961, as it weighed two-thirds less than the previous unit. The new radios found use on stakeouts and at other times officers needed communication away from their patrol cars. Two units could receive each other for a range of up to 1 mile, unless they were relayed through the headquarters radio room. (*Charlotte Observer.*)

Police communicators continued to manually assign calls for service into the mid-1970s. In 1973, they handled 600,000 calls from the public and had to keep track of the locations of up to 100 patrol cars. At that time, dispatchers took a call, filled out a paper form, looked up census tract information by hand, used maps to determine what cars were in the area of the call, and then radioed the officer in the field. The process from call to dispatch took an average of four minutes, with the time from dispatch to an officer's arrival on the scene taking another four minutes. (*Charlotte Observer.*)

In 1975, Charlotte police began using a new $410,000 computerized dispatch system—the first department in the Carolinas to embrace the new technology. This equipment allowed police dispatchers to send cars to the scene of an emergency an average of two minutes faster than the old manual process. The new system utilized computerized forms, automatically selected the police car in the best position to respond, and checked to see if the address given by the caller existed and if there was a history of trouble at that address. The whole procedure now took merely seconds, but a dispatcher still had to relay all that information to the officer in the field over the radio. (*Charlotte Observer.*)

A dispatcher stays alert during a late-night shift at the department communications center in April 1988. (*Charlotte Observer.*)

Charlotte officer D. B. Wright demonstrates one of the Mobile Data Terminals (MDTs) police began installing in patrol cars in 1988. These units saved time by reducing the use of radio communications to dispatching police to calls. Furthermore, they allowed officers to run drivers' licenses, plates, and other records. Laptop computers have now replaced these early units. (*Charlotte Observer.*)

In 2009, CMPD telecommunicators, including Wayne Watkins (above), handled more than 1 million calls, processing them on Vesta Intelligent Workstations. This system allows instant audio recording and displays the telephone number and location of callers, even pinpointing calls originating on cellular sources. The system also recognizes non-voice communication devices used by speech- and hearing-impaired persons. (CMPD Archives.)

# *Ten*

# Taking Doors and Chasing Bad Guys

## Courage in the Line of Duty

Most police officers will tell you that police work is fairly boring—except when it is not.

The courageous task of responding to dangerous situations is the duty of both regular line officers and those belonging to specially trained units. It falls to police to deal with civil unrest, apprehend violent criminals, and peacefully diffuse high-risk situations before they become deadly.

Sometimes the demands on those called to serve have been great. As of 2009, twenty-seven police belonging to the Charlotte, Mecklenburg, and Charlotte-Mecklenburg police have given their lives in pursuit of their ideals. Many more officers have been injured.

Around midnight on August 25, 1919, Charlotte police chief Walter B. Orr, in command of 30 police officers and about 50 armed strikebreakers, faced a crowd of striking streetcar workers and North Charlotte mill-hands at the streetcar maintenance facility on the corner of Bland Street and South Boulevard. Around 1:00 a.m., a scuffle broke out when the strikers demanded the identity of a police officer who had beaten a youth earlier in the evening. As the crowd surged forward, Orr was heard to shout, "Get back, every damn one of you." A maintenance worker on duty later stated that Orr's warning effectively turned the crowd, which began to run away. Police opened fire. Orr claimed in trial testimony the first shot came from the crowd, though other sources assert the strikers were unarmed. More than 100 shots rang out, killing five strikers and wounding about a dozen more. Dilworth residents described the sound as "like from a machine gun." (CMPD Archives.)

Mecklenburg police bust an illegal liquor operation around 1942. Police had lots of time to get good at chasing local bootleggers. North Carolina initially became a dry state in 1909. Even after federal Prohibition ended in 1933 and independent counties were given the "local option" to repeal the earlier state law, Mecklenburg stayed dry and continued to forbid liquor sales until 1947. (CMPD Archives.)

As tensions began to rise in the mid-1960s, some local officers began receiving special training to deal with civil disturbances. Initially, 14 officers under the command of O. A. Crenshaw Jr. made up the department's riot squad. Organizers thought the squad's unusual appearance—with blue helmets and nickel-plated shotguns, complete with bayonets—added psychological support in breaking up riots. Here the riot squad practices moving a crowd back. (*Charlotte Observer.*)

Here a Charlotte patrolman practices dispersing a chemical agent. This technique effectively works to break up crowds without the types of tragic consequences that marred the 1919 streetcar workers' strike and other early-20th-century labor disturbances. (*Charlotte Observer.*)

Patrolman M. C. Moore demonstrates a department .45 submachine gun in February 1968. This is the type of weapon that can bring a quick resolution to a situation, but one that police hope they never need to employ. In 1974, Moore became commander of the department's first SWAT team. (*Charlotte Observer.*)

Policemen collect themselves after a gun battle that broke out at 1530 South Church Street on December 20, 1964. The homeowner, drunk and in a highly agitated state, began the incident by blasting a shotgun at his wife, injuring her, two of their children, and a neighbor. Charlotte patrolmen Harry T. Jones and Rufus W. Hamilton responded and were fired upon and hit shortly after they arrived. Hamilton, the less seriously injured officer, spun upon being shot in the back, drew his service weapon, and fired at the suspect, hitting him in the side. The assailant died on his porch before backup officers arrived on the scene. (*Charlotte Observer.*)

Four city policemen subdue a man who, on March 30, 1964, allegedly walked into a house on the 100 block of Annette Street and began shooting with a handgun, striking his wife in the abdomen with one of the bullets. (*Charlotte Observer.*)

In the wake of Martin Luther King Jr.'s assassination, Charlotte and Mecklenburg police mobilized quickly to prevent the violence that gripped other cities. When a crowd of 75 people gathered at the square on April 6, 1968, and shattered a plate-glass window, police moved in swinging wooden clubs and sent the crowd running down Trade Street. (*Charlotte Observer.*)

Police downed this man in the entrance of a West Trade Street clothing store just after the glass-breaking incident. They struck at him as he ran down the street but were not seen to strike him after he fell. (*Charlotte Observer.*)

When Charlotte-Mecklenburg schools began busing for integration in the 1970s, racially motivated disruptions, including bomb threats, vandalism, and violence, occurred regularly at many schools. Beleaguered administrators often called on police to restore order. (*Charlotte Observer.*)

Officers often enter into dangerous situations in the name of duty. Here a city patrolman, with his service weapon drawn, searches for a bank robbery suspect thought to be hiding at the Edgehill Terrace Apartments in June 1979. (*Charlotte Observer.*)

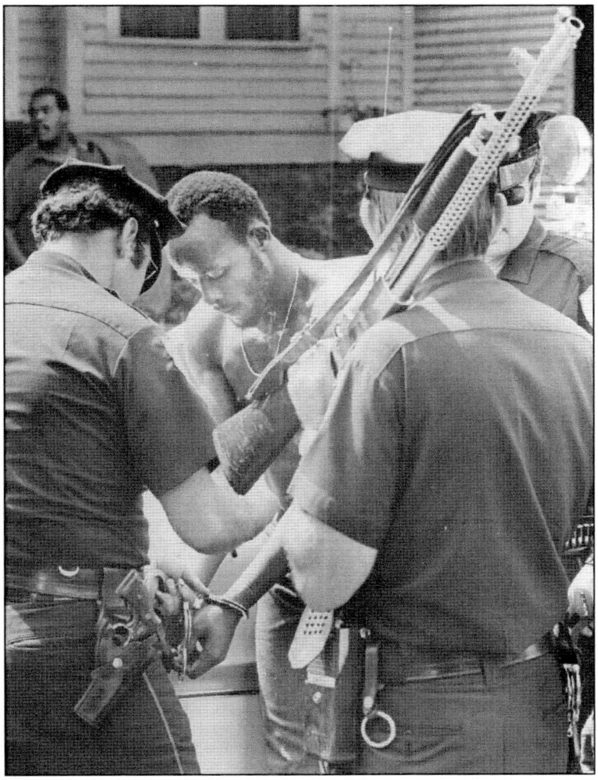

Police take as few chances as possible when it comes to arresting dangerous fugitives. Here Charlotte police take into custody a suspect in the 1974 robbery of the Dial Finance Company. The officer with the shotgun is M. L. Helms. (*Charlotte Observer.*)

Officer R. C. "Butch" Hutchins became covered in construction site mud while chasing several suspects believed to have robbed a grocery store and to have shot Officer H. L. Kuchenbrod. Police caught all of them. (CMPD Archives.)

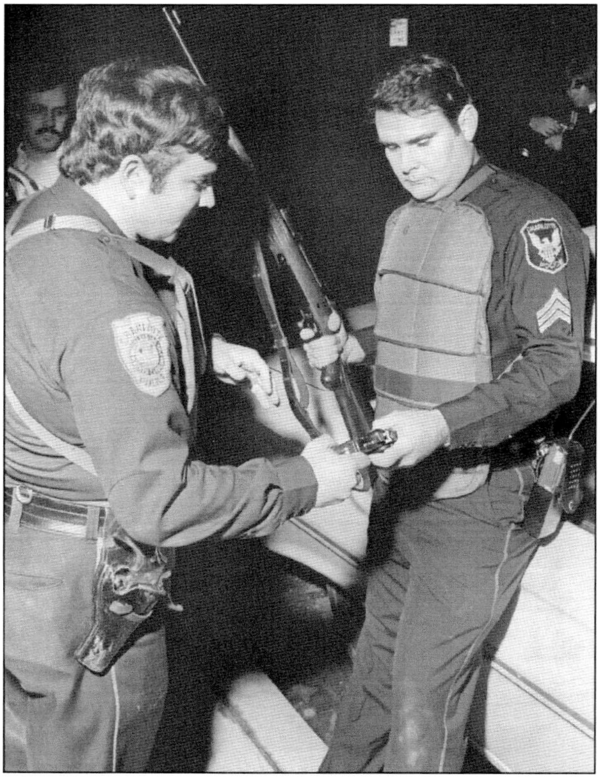

On January 4, 1975, SWAT sniper Sgt. J. J. Kelley (right) received much notoriety after shooting a .357 Magnum revolver from a woman's hand during a hostage situation at the Simpson Bonding Company on North Myers Street. Officer Walter Dunn, the first team member to rush the building (left), picked up the pistol and shows it to Sergeant Kelly. (*Charlotte Observer.*)

County patrolman Ray Trull fires a tear-gas canister into a house on Capps Hill Mine Road during the climax of a four-hour siege in the mid-1970s. (*Charlotte Observer.*)

A Mecklenburg County officer prepares to enter the home of an enraged gunman after police have deployed chemical agents in 1974. The suspect surrendered just before police were to storm the gas-filled residence. (*Charlotte Observer.*)

Officer Paul A. Roseboro (center) and other members of the Charlotte SWAT team disarm after the resolution of a situation in which a troubled youth took nine hostages at a home for unwed mothers. After 10 intense hours, the suspect gave himself up to police. (*Charlotte Observer.*)

Members of the SWAT team constantly train so, when activated, their skills are sharply honed. Here SWAT officer Rich Boyer takes aim with a shotgun adapted to fire chemical agents during a 1982 training exercise. (*Charlotte Observer.*)

When a gunman took over a home on Sardis Road in September 1984 and refused to surrender, the SWAT team moved into position, using a fire truck as cover. (*Charlotte Observer*.)

SWAT sniper J. D. Cox is in position on an airport rooftop above Air Force One in the 1990s. (*Charlotte Observer*.)

The department bought its first tactical vehicle in 1966—an old armored car formerly used to haul money. Chief John Hord had the car outfitted with a new engine and paint job. Additionally, police added a loudspeaker, shotguns, machine guns, tear-gas grenades, gas masks, and other emergency equipment. The *Charlotte Observer* described the new vehicle as "big and black and mean looking. Impregnable, like a mother-in-law." In all, it only cost about $500. (*Charlotte Observer*.)

One tool available to the CMPD SWAT team is the Dragoon Armored Rescue Vehicle, seen here participating in a terrorism response exercise. As of 2009, eight officers are assigned to the vehicle and are trained in all areas of its maintenance and operation. (CMPD Archives.)

Police would prefer to end hostage situations peacefully; violent resolutions pose extreme risks to police, the hostages, the suspect, and any innocent bystanders who may catch a stray bullet. Diffusing such situations peacefully requires persons of extreme skill. One such officer was department veteran Cheryl Horner, seen here on the scene of a nine-hour standoff that she worked with Officer Roy House in late December 1987. The officers successfully got the suspect to release his three hostages and peacefully give himself up. (*Charlotte Observer.*)

Charlotte police hostage negotiators Sgt. Tim Stewart and Officer Ricki Becker speak to reporters in September 1984. The two officers successfully negotiated the release of a hostage during an 18-hour standoff, but ultimately, the gunman shot himself. "We didn't have any control over what that man did," said Stewart. "We tried to talk him out of it, and I'm sorry that we didn't. I wish he hadn't killed himself, but he's the one who pulled the trigger." (*Charlotte Observer.*)

With the help of federal funding and access to military training, the Charlotte police established a bomb squad in 1971 to be responsible for the handling, transportation, and rendering of safe explosive items. Officer W. G. Burnette and Sgt. F. P. Toomey became the department's first two bomb specialists. Since its inception, the unit has grown increasingly sophisticated in its use of specialized equipment, including armored suits, X-ray machines, water cannons, and even robots. (*Charlotte Observer.*)

One of the earliest tools purchased by the newly formed unit was this Colt bomb containment transport trailer. This tool allowed officers to remove suspect explosives safely from populated

Officer Ron Hayes examines a briefcase located next to the body of man found dead at I-77 and Clanton Road in January 1985. Later police determined the man most likely froze to death. (*Charlotte Observer.*)

areas. Here officers use a line to lower a suitcase thought to contain a bomb from a bank before driving it 18 miles away and blowing it up in March 1981. (*Charlotte Observer.*)

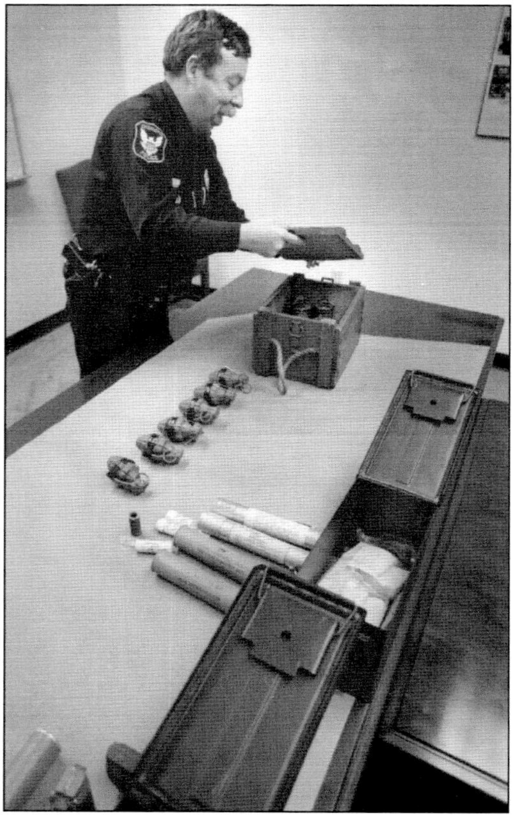

Bomb squad member Don Penix organizes grenades and other military ordinance seized after the January 1993 arrest of a suspect. (*Charlotte Observer.*)

A bomb squad member in a protective suit carefully approaches the suspect case prior to detonating it. (*Charlotte Observer.*)

City police bomb squad members examine X-ray negatives to determine if a briefcase left by a telephone booth in March 1993 at the corner of South Tryon Street and Kingston Avenue contained a bomb. (*Charlotte Observer.*)

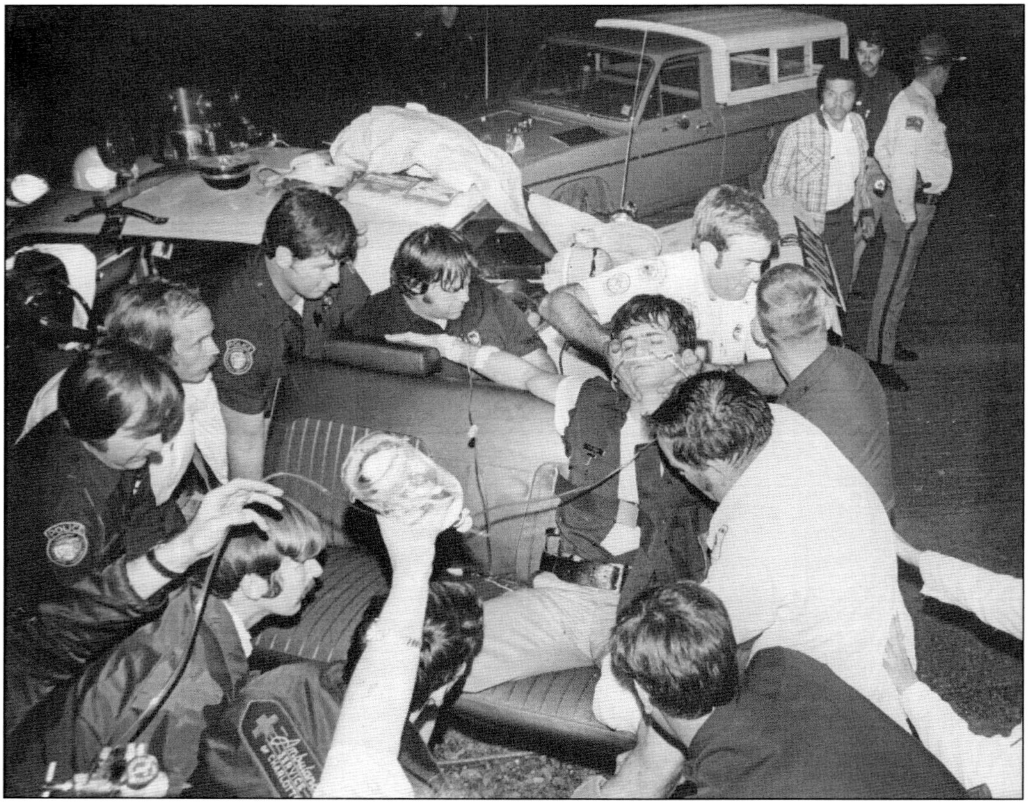

Medics and police work to move Mecklenburg County patrolman Bobby Ray Pence to a waiting ambulance in October 1975. Pence and his partner were driving along an unfinished gravel portion of I-77 toward Huntersville when they hit a 35-foot-long metal reinforcement rod that ripped through the patrol car and impaled Pence to his seat. The painful ordeal lasted two hours as rescuers cut the rod and parts of the car apart in order to remove the front seat and extract the officer safely. (*Charlotte Observer.*)

Emotions overcome Officer Doug F. Martin at the scene of the shooting of fellow officer Tim Whittington, slain by a burglary suspect on July 16, 1985. (*Charlotte Observer.*)

On June 5, 1973, Officers J. C. Stanton and L. D. Walker responded to what appeared to be a routine domestic disturbance call, only to encounter a crazed man who viciously attacked both officers. The suspect shrugged off blows from nightsticks, disarmed both officers of their clubs, and grabbed Stanton's service revolver after slamming the officer's head into the patrol car's bumper. (*Charlotte Observer.*)

As they struggled, the suspect shot Stanton five times, the final bullet slamming into the officer's badge. Walker fired two bullets into the suspect's chest, which only made him laugh and then attempt to rip a shotgun from the officer's patrol car. Two more bullets from Walker's gun ended the struggle. (*Charlotte Observer.*)

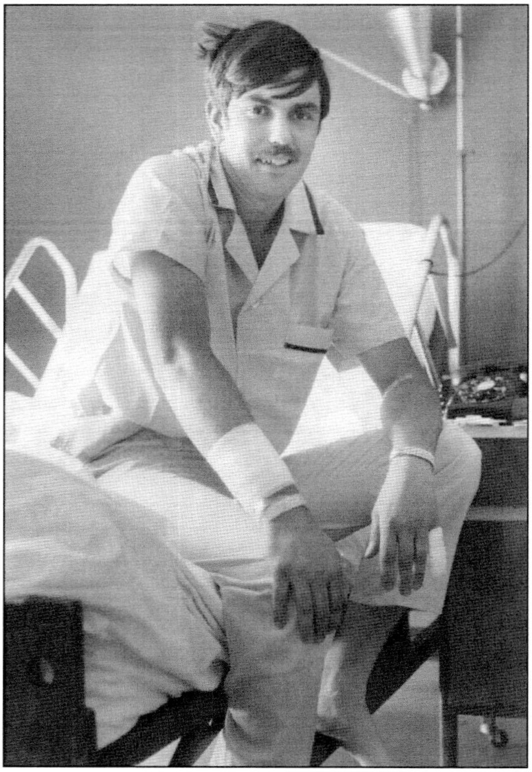

Stanton recovered from his gunshot wounds and for years carried the badge that likely saved his life. Sadly, Walker became partially paralyzed in his left arm when he received treatment after the incident; a hospital worker's injection damaged a nerve, limiting his duties for the next three years. Both officers remained with the department. (*Charlotte Observer.*)

In this 1981 photograph, slain officer Ed Cannon's nine-year-old son holds the flag that draped his father's casket. (*Charlotte Observer.*)

# *Eleven*

# Tackling Traffic Safety
## Protecting the Public on the Roads

While the streets of Charlotte were often busy and congested during the wagon and buggy days, the sudden proliferation of automobiles on city streets and Mecklenburg roads in the early 20th century forever changed the role of police in maintaining public safety.

Car ownership in Charlotte increased from under 2,000 to more than 20,000 between 1917 and 1925. Suddenly, officers had to deal with controlling traffic flow, enforcing speed laws, arresting intoxicated and reckless drivers, pursuing getaway vehicles used in crimes, intercepting the transportation of contraband, and reconstructing automobile crashes.

ISTORICAL PAGEANT OF MECKLENBURG
MAY 18 - 22
BLAKE'S
DRUGS
NORRIS
CANDIES
MELLON
MEN, WOMEN & BOYS
CO.

Chief Walter Orr established the South's first traffic signal system at the square in 1918. Originally, it turned on a hand-crank system from the ground but was shortly thereafter operated from a tower on the square's southwest corner. Seen here in the 1920s, the control tower also contained a sign totaling the city's traffic deaths for the year. (PLCMC, Carolina Room.)

A Charlotte police officer on a Harley-Davidson Servi-Car (a three-wheeled motorcycle) marks car tires with chalk around 1939. When the patrolman returns after a prescribed period of time, he will know which cars to ticket for exceeding the parking zone's time limit. (City of Charlotte.)

Booting the wheel of a car, seen here in March 1956, immobilizes the offensively parked vehicle, thus ensuring that violators pay their fines before going home. (*Charlotte Observer.*)

Here Officer Jack Wallace (left) employs a "whammy" to check speeds in the early 1950s. This device made use of two rubber hoses stretched perpendicularly across the road and set apart at a fixed distance. The connected box measured the time taken for the vehicle to travel between the hoses. Radar did not come into widespread use until the late 1960s. (CMPD Archives.)

This city patrolman has drawn the difficult assignment of directing traffic at the square during a November 1964 snowstorm. Working during inclement weather is difficult and requires officers to be extra alert. (*Charlotte Observer.*)

The 1949 opening of Charlotte's first urban highway project, the Independence Boulevard cross-town expressway, radically changed how traffic in Charlotte worked. The thoroughfare cut a swath through the city, breaking up Charlotte's grid system of lights and intersections to provide motorists an express route to the southern edges of the city. More lanes handling a greater number of motorists traveling at higher speeds brought new challenges for the Charlotte police. Here a city patrolman bravely directs traffic on Independence Boulevard in the late 1960s. (*Charlotte Observer.*)

The economic prosperity in the years following World War II allowed many more Charlotteans the means to purchase automobiles. Such a marked increase in the numbers of motorists on the road meant more automobile-related duties for local law enforcement. (*Charlotte Observer*.)

Officers measure skid marks as part of the reconstruction of a fatal October 1962 accident. (*Charlotte Observer*.)

In a 1988 cost-effective effort to curb speeding, stop sign, and red light violations, Charlotte police borrowed this mannequin from the Ivey's department store and pressed her into service at trouble spots. If motorists seemed to be catching on to "Officer Dolly" in a given area, police switched her out with a real officer to write tickets. The idea came from the department's success in years past with leaving empty cars near the homes of known bootleggers to discourage customers from buying. (*Charlotte Observer.*)

Radar speed trailers are one way police encourage motorists to check their speed and voluntarily comply with the limit. (CMPD Archives.)

# ACKNOWLEDGMENTS

It is said, "He who stands on the shoulders of giants, sees furthest of all." All students of the past benefit from the writings of previous historians, journalists, collectors, archivists, librarians, and people who rescue history from trash cans. Rarely, too, is a project of this scope an individual effort, and many colleagues deserve a word of thanks for their assistance.

The work of local historians Thomas W. Hanchett, David Goldfield, Dan Morrill, Mary Kratt, and LeGette Blythe both inspired me as a historian and influenced this volume's content. I also owe a debt of gratitude to Charlotte antiquarians of long ago, such as Daniel Augustus Tompkins, Dr. John Brevard Alexander, and Dr. Charles M. Strong, who persevered in their writings so much that would otherwise be lost to history. As always, the staff at the public library's Carolina Room proved invaluable and offered much insight and assistance—especially Sheila Bumgarner and Jane Johnson.

Journalists write history's first draft. I am especially appreciative to the writers and photographers who covered crime and policing for our media; the largest sources of information for this book were the pages of local newspapers. I would especially like to thank Bert Fox, June Lancaster, Marion Paynter, and Maria David at the *Charlotte Observer* for granting us access to their photographic holdings for this project.

Many officers and non-sworn personnel within their departments have made great efforts to preserve police history—there are many more than I can name here. Officer Eloise Brown maintained the department's collection of photographs for many years through the mid-20th century. Lt. J. R. Hall authored a pamphlet on the history of the Charlotte Police Department in 1966. Furthermore, a team of officers and staff headed by Darrellyn Kiser and Patty Beatty collected and published much Charlotte PD history in a 1990 yearbook. Detective Dan Cunius dedicated countless hours researching the histories of the officers killed in the line of duty. Deputy Chief Harold Medlock formed a committee of CMPD officers interested in preserving the history of the department, which benefited from the valued participation of Sgt. Tom Barry and Officer Eric Boulware. I also greatly valued the input of Officer Christopher P. Eubanks and retired sergeants Bud Cesena and J. D. Cox. None of this would have been possible without the support of chief of police Rodney Monroe.

This book is based on the exhibit Behind the Badge: Policing in Charlotte and Mecklenburg County, 1865–2009. The CMPD Benevolent Fund sponsored the adaptation. The fund is a nonprofit organization that provides financial assistance to CMPD employees during a personal crisis or hardship. Mary Davis Smart and the staff of the Charlotte Museum of History oversaw the project, which was run out of CMPD's Research and Planning Division, directed by Paul Paskoff. Melissa Manware Treadaway managed the entire CMPD History initiative, beginning with building up and professionalizing the department's own historic archive and artifact collections and seeing the exhibit through to completion.

# Selected Bibliography

The largest sources informing this volume are the original coverage of these events as presented in the *Charlotte Observer*, *Charlotte News*, and other local media; Charlotte and Mecklenburg Records; and the recollection of those present. The following books provided a great deal of valuable information and helped contextualize the story of policing inside the greater story of our community.


Alexander, J. B. *The History of Mecklenburg County From 1740 to 1900*. Charlotte, NC: Charlotte Observer Printing House, 1902.

Bradbury, Tom. *Dilworth: The First 100 Years*. Charlotte, NC: Dilworth Community Development Association, 1992.

Brockmann, Legette, and Charles Raven Blythe. *Hornets' Nest: The Story of Charlotte and Mecklenburg County*. Charlotte, NC: Mcnally of Charlotte, 1961.

Dulaney, W. Marvin. *Black Police in America (Blacks in the Diaspora)*. Bloomington, IN: Indiana University Press, 1996.

Greenwood, Janette Thomas. *Bittersweet Legacy: The Black and White "Better Classes" in Charlotte, 1850–1910*. Chapel Hill, NC: The University of North Carolina Press, 2001.

Hadden, Sally E. *Slave Patrols: Law and Violence in Virginia and the Carolinas (Harvard Historica Studies)*. Cambridge, MA: Harvard University Press, 2003.

Hanchett, Thomas W., and Ryan L. Sumner. *Charlotte and the Carolina Piedmont*. Charleston, SC: Arcadia Publishing, 2003.

Hanchett, Thomas W. *Sorting Out the New South City: Race, Class, and Urban Development in Charlotte, 1875–1975*. Chapel Hill, NC: The University of North Carolina Press, 1998.

Kiser, D., et al. *Charlotte Police Department, 1866–1991*, Dallas, TX: Taylor Publishing Company, 1990.

Kratt, Mary Norton. *New South Women: Twentieth Century Women of Charlotte, North Carolina*. Winston-Salem, NC: John F. Blair Publisher, 2001.

Morrill, Dr. Dan L. *Historic Charlotte: An Illustrated History of Charlotte & Mecklenburg County*. San Antonio, TX: Historical Pub Network, 2002.

Tompkins, D. A. *History of Mecklenburg County and the City of Charlotte from 1740 to 1903. 2 Volumes*. Charlotte, NC: Observer Printing House, 1903.

Wertheimer, John W. *Law and Society in the South: A History of North Carolina Court Cases (New Directions in Southern History)*. Lexington, KY: University Press of Kentucky, 2009.

Yandle, Mary Lois Moore. *The Spirit of a Proud People: Pictures and Stories of Highland Park Manufacturing Mill #3 and the People in the Village of North Charlotte*. Charlotte, NC: L. M. Yandle, 1997.